CREATIVE PROBLEM SOLVING

An Introduction

Third Edition

CREATIVE PROBLEM SOLVING

An Introduction

Third Edition

Donald J. Treffinger
Scott G. Isaksen • K. Brian Dorval

Published in cooperation with
Center for Creative Learning, Inc.

Copyright © 2000 Center for Creative Learning and
Creative Problem Solving Group—Buffalo

Graphic Production: Libby Lindsey

ISBN 1-882664-62-0

PRUFROCK PRESS
P.O. Box 8813
Waco, TX 76714-8813
Phone: (800) 998-2208
Fax: (800) 240-0333
www.prufrock.com

Contents

Figures

Figure

Tables

Table

Authors' Foreword

Creative Problem Solving has passed many tests. It has withstood the scrutiny of research and scholarly review, and it has been described by independent investigators as one of the strongest approaches for structured problem solving. It has passed the test of breadth and generalizability, across many different settings and age levels from childhood through adult. It has stood the important tests of time and use. For nearly four decades since Osborn's pioneering publications, CPS is one of the longest standing frameworks for practical application. This historical record might lead one to believe that CPS must surely be rigidly prescribed, perhaps by now even suffering from stiffness or resistance to change that is often born of endurance. Such assumptions will be quickly dispatched by even a casual investigation of growth and changes in CPS over time.

We make no claims now, nor have we ever, to having "invented" CPS. We have always emphasized that our vision arises only from "standing on the shoulders" of many colleagues of considerable stature. We have always described ourselves explicitly as members of the third generation of colleagues. Those whose ideas, experiences, and research have enriched our thought and practice, along with thousands of others like us throughout the world, were named and discussed in our previous works. We still thank them. Our appreciation of their contributions is undiminished. They include Alex F. Osborn (whose work started the entire tradition), Ruth Noller, Sid Parnes, E. Paul Torrance, Don MacKinnon, Cal Taylor, and J. P. Guilford. Many new names might be added to our list of people to thank. We must express our appreciation to our associates at the Creative Problem Solving Group—Buffalo and the Center for Creative Learning, to our clients and partners in numerous schools, corporations, and other organizations throughout the world, and to our many colleagues in academic settings.

We do claim, as a goal as much as an assertion, that our generation—ourselves, our contemporary colleagues, and the emerging colleagues (many of whom are or were initially our graduate students or clients)—continues to move forward in understanding CPS and its applications. CPS today is different from "the process," as it was described in 1953, 1967, or 1977. It also differs in many important ways from its form and structure when we wrote *Creative Problem Solving: The Basic Course* in 1985 or the first edition of *Creative Approaches to Problem Solving* in 1994. This book presents our newest, most contemporary approach in which we continue our efforts to build on current research and to make CPS natural, descriptive, and "user friendly." We believe that readers who know previous presentations of CPS will find this version familiar, friendly, and forward-looking. We hope this book will help readers to master the basics of CPS. Please let us know how you are continuing to apply and modify CPS, so it will continue to be an expanding, growing framework for the future.

—Donald J. Treffinger, Scott G. Isaksen, and K. Brian Dorval

Preface

It has been said that, "We cannot direct the winds, but we can set our sails to gather the winds that steer our course." Don Treffinger, Scott Isaksen, and Brian Dorval are individuals who have directed the sails of their educational careers to gather the winds of creativity. They are ever sincerely working toward helping others to realize the tremendous potential that those people hold within themselves, which can be realized through the effective application of Creative Problem Solving (CPS).

During the past 30 years or so, which fairly well define my career in the world of creativity, there has surely been no dearth of publications in the field. All manner and means of manuals, texts, workbooks, research, project reports, and the like have been published in an attempt to inform the general public and "professionals" alike about this elusive subject. The concept of creativity is mysterious to some people, challenging to others, scoffed at and held in disdain by some, but it provides direction for the life's work of others. For Don and Scott, and now for Brian as well, it has been an intellectual challenge and a focal point for scholarship, teaching, and training.

This book is the authors' latest effort to provide a better understanding of CPS, an integral part of the world of creativity, and it is exemplary in its presentation. So often I am asked for a reference that offers a concise, well-documented, easily read description of CPS for individuals or groups to use (on their own or with experienced guidance). *Creative Problem Solving: An Introduction* provides exactly that. It offers a fresh look at some of the "time-honored" techniques of CPS in an easygoing, almost conversational, format. Some of the guidelines for following the process, which are often emphasized in instructor-led sessions but often only implied in written materials, are made more explicit here.

It is an honor for me to preface this work, and I do so with a challenge to all readers:

Try it! I believe you'll not only enjoy it, but you'll profit from it in ways you presently wouldn't imagine! You have an unknown strength of creativity within you ... that can be realized more fully if you will set your sails to gather the potential energy offered within these pages.

—Dr. Ruth B. Noller,
Distinguished Service Professor, Emeritus
State University College at Buffalo

Chapter 1
An Overview of CPS

You should read this book if you've ever found yourself in a situation in which you needed to define or understand the nature of a problem, think up some new ideas, or devise and carry out an action plan. You will probably protest, "But everyone has been in those situations, time and time again, in everyday life!" Exactly! To be successful, everyone needs to be able to identify and solve problems. Creative Problem Solving (which we will simply refer to as CPS in this book) is a process anyone can use to deal with many of life's everyday problems, opportunities, and challenges, such as:

- "I'd like to attract more customers for my business."

- "My new invention would really be useful to people if I could find a clever way to market it."

- "How can I attract the attention of that great redhead in my world history class?"

- "We need to get some new program ideas so our organization's members will attend our meetings."

- "I wish our family would find enjoyable ways to spend more time together."

- "I wish I had ways to help my students be more excited or motivated about learning."

- "I'm looking for ways to empower people to take more responsibility for quality and improvement."

How do you feel when you have to deal with any of these situations, or others like them? Excited? Eager? Or, frustrated and tense? Do you believe that you can come up with ideas that are as good as anyone else's (and perhaps even better), or are you easily discouraged?

If you have always thought that only a few very special people—real geniuses—can come up with creative ideas, you have most likely been underestimating your own powers of thinking and doing. We believe that everyone has the ability to think creatively and critically, and that everyone can be successful in solving problems effectively and productively. Unfortunately, left to themselves, not everyone will use the mental power that is easily within their reach. But, anyone can!

By learning and applying the simple, easy-to-use methods and techniques in this book, you will soon see improvements in your own thinking and problem solving. This is a book to help anyone be more creatively productive; it's not about creativity as a form of rare "genius" beyond the reach of most people. This book provides an overview of a systematic approach to Creative Problem Solving (CPS), building upon and extending our own prior work (e.g., Treffinger, Isaksen, & Firestien, 1982, 1983; Isaksen & Treffinger, 1985; Isaksen, Dorval, & Treffinger, 1994) and that of our colleagues (e.g., Firestien, 1988; Osborn, 1953; Parnes, 1967, 1981; Parnes, Noller, & Biondi, 1977). By learning and using CPS, you will increase your ability to:

1. recognize opportunities, challenges and concerns;

2. examine data in your situation to discover the most important challenge at the heart of the situation;

3. consider many ways to state the problem, and then select a specific problem statement that will stimulate ideas;

4. generate many, varied, and unusual ideas for dealing with the problem you've stated;

5. identify and use tools for choosing, analyzing, and developing promising ideas;

6. examine promising possible solutions and then plan for successful implementation; and

7. design and carry out a specific and detailed plan of action.

Think of CPS as a "toolbox" to help you organize your own creative and critical thinking and problem-solving abilities, and to insure that the tools you need are handy and ready when you need them. These tools have been drawn from observation and experience with the productive thinking and problem-solving methods people use naturally. They also incorporate the findings of many years of research about the characteristics and skills of creative persons and from knowledge of creative processes and products in many fields. CPS has been used successfully by many people—adults, teenagers, children, in school, at home, and at work—since the mid-1950s. Every CPS method or tool in this book has been used successfully in real life.

We use the word *tool* quite specifically and deliberately in this book, and a word of explanation might be helpful. We are concerned that, in the area of creativity and thinking skills, a number of terms are often used inconsistently and sometimes carelessly (as though they were all interchangeable, when actually they are not). We ought to strive together to make our common vocabulary in the field more precise, concise, and consistent.

Three terms, *tool*, *strategy*, and *technique*, are excellent examples of the situation. You will find that they are used freely and not at all carefully throughout the literature (and we discovered that we have been as guilty of this as anyone else). For this book, then, we have made an effort to be more careful and consistent in using these terms.

A *tool* is a specific device that aids in accomplishing any task or operation. (If you are playing golf, for example, the clubs in your golf bag and a generous supply of golf balls are tools that you will need.) Your *strategy* is your working plan, continuously being monitored and carried out for choosing and using the tools you need to accomplish your goal. The strategy involves asking what tool or tools you need at a certain time and understanding why they might be the most appropriate tools for what needs to be done. (In golf, you probably won't step up to the first tee with your putter in hand, nor use a nine iron for that final three-foot putt.) Finally, *technique* has to do with how you use the tool(s) you have selected. There are often many ways to use any tools, not just one "right or wrong" way. (In the golf example, technique might involve the grip, the placement of your arms, legs, and head, the swing or stroke, and the follow through.)

As you work with CPS, you will learn many different tools. Some of them, such as brainstorming, are tools for generating ideas, while others, such as an evaluation matrix, are tools to help you focus your thinking. Questions of strategy will address when you might want to use one tool or another and why. You will discover that all of these "tools for the mind" can be used in different ways to accommodate different situations, needs, or personal styles. For more information about our use of these three terms, you might read Treffinger (1997) or Isaksen, Dorval, and Treffinger (1998).

Since this is not a technical, academic textbook, we will avoid long theoretical explanations or detailed descriptions of research studies. Concise summaries of much of the research evidence regarding the impact and effectiveness of CPS can be found in reviews by Isaksen, Dorval, and Treffinger (1994), Isaksen and DeSchryver (2000), Isaksen, Treffinger, and Dorval (1997), Torrance (1972, 1987), Parnes (1987), and Rose and Lin (1984). In addition to these reviews, several other specific articles providing evidence for the effectiveness of CPS are also included in the bibliography at the end of this book. An extensive bibliography can also be downloaded from http://www.creativelearning.com on the Internet.

Misconceptions About Creativity

We should deal with several common misunderstandings about creativity, so they will be out of your way from the very beginning.

Myth 1. I am not a creative person. Because many people think of creativity as a rare or special quality possessed only by a few exceptional geniuses, it is often much too easy for them to be overly doubtful or hesitant of their own creative potential. To the contrary, we view creativity as an important aspect of everyday living—the potential for anyone to be able to think of new and useful ideas, to look at a problem in a new way and find an original and workable solution, to use one's mind in a productive way to generate and apply new ideas.

Myth 2. Creativity is too mysterious to be taught. Some people believe that creativity is a very esoteric phenomenon—a visit by a muse, a divine gift, or an unpredictable and uncontrollable moment of inspiration. Viewing creativity as mysterious takes it out of the realm of "mere mortal" behavior and makes it seem supernatural. In such a view, it is unlikely that creativity can be studied scientifically or nurtured—and perhaps even risky to attempt to do so, at risk of disturbing the forces that control creativity, or frightening away the muse. In contrast, we believe that creativity is best viewed as natural and observable. Many methods and techniques for enhancing creative productivity are rational, powerful, and accessible to anyone who desires to learn and use them.

Myth 3. Creativity equals arts. Another common misunderstanding views creativity only in relation to people, efforts, or outcomes in the fine arts. It is not unusual, for example, for people to say to us, "Oh, I'm not very creative; I'm not much of an artist [or a musician, or a poet …]." To be sure, creativity in the arts is very real, and it adds a great deal to the quality of human life. But creativity does not occur only in the arts; it can be seen in any area of human endeavor. Creativity exists wherever and whenever people direct their efforts toward new or original ideas, expanding or refining important parts of their life and surroundings, or solving ambiguous, novel, or complex problems.

Myth 4. Creativity as madness. For some people, the word *creativity* evokes the image of the wild, crazy, eccentric person, or the cartoon caricature of the "mad scientist." Despite the fact that such views—"the fine line" between genius and insanity, for example—have been debunked for decades, they still reappear quite consistently in many discussions of creativity. We believe that a person functioning creatively is, in fact, operating in ways that can lead to personal effectiveness and good health.

We cannot forget that creativity is a very complex phenomenon, understood by many people in many different ways (e.g., Isaksen, Murdock, Firestien, & Treffinger, 1993a, 1993b). As a result, these misunderstandings—and many others—will always be likely to arise in any group in which creativity is a topic of discussion. For our present purposes, we hope these four examples of myths and misunderstandings will be sufficient. We hope, as you consider them carefully, they will help you highlight for yourself the important message that creativity is not strange and far removed from each of us as we proceed through life. It is not an exotic concept, or a weird maladaptation of human behavior. Creativity is a natural, understandable, and manageable process through which anyone can become a more productive thinker.

The Importance of Creativity

It is easy to get comfortable in life's patterns—the things we do the same way all the time that bring stability, order, and predictability to life from one day to another. There was a time when we all thought we knew what the future would be like and what we would need to know to keep up with things. We knew what would be necessary to be educated, well-informed, cultured, happy, and successful, and we felt we could simply pass that important knowledge along from one generation to another.

Unfortunately, our long-range vision has not been very good, and things have not really worked out in that neat, simple, easily manageable way. In the late 1800s, for example, the Director of the U.S. Patent Office is said to have predicted his office would soon close, because "everything that would ever need to be invented had already been made!" In the early part of the 20th century, some "experts" also proclaimed that the entire space science effort was a waste of time and money, because it was simply foolish to think that anyone would ever be able to leave the Earth's surface or, in the most outrageous fantasy, that any human would ever walk on the surface of the moon. Many things are quite different today than anyone previously thought they might be.

Exercise: Then—and Now!

Before you continue reading, please pause for a few moments to try the exercise below. Write down some of your reactions to the question in the exercise before you resume reading again.

Consider how many things have changed in your own life experience since your childhood. Ask yourself, "What do children today take for granted—accept as an ordinary, everyday part of their life—that I did not even imagine when I was their age?" List below some of the common things today that didn't exist when you were a child:

_____

_____

_____

_____

_____

Here are some of the common responses we have heard when we have asked this question to groups in seminars or training programs:

- computers and calculators;
- microwave ovens;
- satellites, satellite dishes, and communications;

- video recorders and compact discs;
- fax machines, photocopiers, and lasers;
- instant, clear, worldwide direct dial phone calls;
- instant photography;
- fast food restaurants;
- rapid transportation (and accessible air travel);
- electronic toys and gadgets of many kinds;
- color television (some people say, "television," and once in awhile, someone says, "radio"); and
- medical advances and reduced hospital stays for many procedures.

Many of these are beneficial, positive aspects of progress (or at least seem so to most people). But, at the same time, people often recognize that there can be a down side to change, too. Pollution has increased, and landfills are becoming overextended. We have created products that we can't seem to dispose of. Resources we once thought were limitless no longer appear to be inexhaustible, creating concern for efficiency and conservation. Competition seems more fierce within the United States and on an international level. The structure and quantity of knowledge is developing at an alarmingly fast pace, so it is becoming almost impossible to be or remain current in any area.

Adaptability, team work, creativity, and imagination are essential for surviving and succeeding. There is little hope or choice for the future other than through continued growing, adapting, changing, creating, or innovating. Despite many difficult obstacles, the study of creativity and innovation is becoming very important for individuals, groups, and organizations.

Any of the methods and tools in this book can be applied to problems or opportunities of individuals, small teams, or large groups. The "client," who is the owner of the problem (i.e., whose problem is the focus for the CPS session), might be either an individual or a group, although, as you will learn, the identity and role of the client should be spelled out explicitly for a successful CPS session to take place. (Incidentally, an individual can apply any CPS methods when working alone on a task, although a group can add both quantity and quality of options.)

Creativity can be important in a number of other ways. It can be important to everyone, at any age, for breaking away from habits that limit us; expanding our vision; doing today's tasks better; discovering new personal opportunities and challenges; enhancing personal health and satisfaction in life; attaining career success and productivity; and expanding the quality and enjoyment of life—for ourselves and others.

Creative and Critical Thinking

What is creative thinking? What is critical thinking? What do they have to do with CPS? There are many different definitions of creativity, creative thinking, and critical thinking, and it would be easy to get bogged down in arguing the merits of one definition or another.

Creative and critical thinking are often seen (or stereotyped) as opposites, poles apart and incompatible. In this view, often supported by some of the misunderstandings described above, the creative thinker is viewed as one who is wild and zany, eccentric or at least a little bit weird or strange, and who thrives on "off the wall" ideas that are usually impractical. On the other hand, the critical thinker is serious, deep, analytical, and impersonal. We believe such stereotypes are neither accurate nor useful. We hold a different view, believing that creative and critical thinking are two complementary, mutually important ways of thinking. They need to work together in harmony. Successful problem solving depends on using both, not just one or the other.

Creative Thinking

Encountering gaps, paradoxes, opportunities, challenges, or concerns; then searching for meaningful new connections by *generating*—

- many possibilities;
- varied possibilities (from different viewpoints or perspectives);
- unusual or original possibilities; and
- details to expand or enrich possibilities.

Creative thinking is often described as a divergent process in which we begin at a single point or with a single question, but extend our search in many different directions, generating a wide variety of new possibilities. We prefer to use the more familiar word *generate* when our goal is to seek many, varied, or unusual possibilities, or to add details and expand on existing possibilities.

Critical Thinking

Examining possibilities carefully, fairly, and constructively; then *focusing* your thoughts and actions by—

- organizing and analyzing possibilities;
- refining and developing promising possibilities;
- ranking or prioritizing options; and
- choosing or deciding on certain options.

Critical thinking is also often called *convergent thinking*, attempting to take many different ideas and draw them together toward a single goal or result. When it is time to shift from generating possibilities in CPS to using critical thinking, we prefer to use the term *focusing*. Think about a camera. Focus is important to bring an image clearly and sharply into view. This is true in thinking, too.

Effective problem solvers must do both—generating and focusing—not just one or the other. Generating many ideas will not be enough by itself to help you solve a problem. Similarly, if you rely only on the focusing side, you may have too few possibilities to choose from. We believe that successful problem solvers can, and do, learn to use both their creative and critical thinking abilities in harmony, generating options and focusing their thinking.

Basic Ground Rules

Our definitions, and all of the methods and tools in this book, actually build on two important principles. These foundations are:

1. When you are generating options, the basic principle to keep in mind is Deferred Judgment.

2. When your attention turns to analyzing, refining, or choosing ideas or options, the second basic principle, Affirmative Judgment, should be used.

Remembering these two basic principles will make it easier for you to understand and use all the specific tools. For each of the two basic principles, there are several important ground rules. These are summarized in Table 1.

Guidelines for Generating Options

Alex Osborn, who introduced and popularized the term *brainstorming* in the 1950s, and upon whose work we still build today, gave us the basic principle of Deferred Judgment, and his rules for brainstorming also have merit today.

We always strive to keep our minds open to all possibilities. Evaluating ideas too quickly often inhibits or squelches ideas. In CPS, we want to avoid any habits or actions that might cause us to overlook or disregard any possibilities, particularly during our initial exploring and searching. There is a time to evaluate new ideas, of course—that's critical to success. It will be very important at other times during the process. But, during periods of generating ideas, evaluation gets in the way. Table 1 summarizes four specific ground rules for generating options:

1. *Defer judgment—separate generating from judging ideas.* When you want to generate options and stretch yourself to search for some new and unique possibilities, evaluation is likely to get in the way. So, the best thing you can do is to let the ideas flow without any criticism or praise. Save the judging and analyzing for later, after you have generated a good, full, rich set of possibilities. During the generating phase, keep the "censors" and judges out of the action (whether they're other people in a group or your own internal censors.) Mixing generating and judging will stifle the flow, so let many options flow freely, writing them all down—and do the judging later!

When Generating Options	When Focusing Options
1. Defer Judgement—separate generating from judging.	1. Affirmative Judgement—use a balanced approach; consider positives as well as negatives.
2. Strive for quantity.	2. Be deliberate and explicit.
3. "Freewheel" and accept all options; strive for unusual possibilities.	3. Consider both novelty and appropriateness.
4. Seek combination.	4. Stay on course.

Table 1: Basic Principles and Ground Rules for CPS

2. *Strive for quantity. Look for lots of options.* Quantity often breeds quality, in that the more you generate, the greater the possibility that at least some of the options will be original and promising for you. Try to express yourself concisely, in just a few words (seek "headlines" or "telegrams," rather than novels—or even short stories!). List the options; don't discuss them. This allows you to use the time that didn't go into long explanations to generate even more alternatives.

3. *"Freewheel" and accept all options.* Capture every thought that comes to mind, without being concerned that some might seem too wild or silly; give yourself permission to be playful. Strive for uniqueness or originality. Sometimes the wildest options might serve as springboards for other new possibilities, for anyone in the group. But, those creative connections might not have been possible if the first, and seemingly silly, thoughts had been held back. As Osborn observed many years ago, it is often easier to tame a wild idea than to breathe excitement into a dull one.

Freewheeling should also remind you of the importance of stretching your mind. It is all too easy for anyone to become mentally lazy, drifting along within the most familiar thoughts and habits, or operating on mental cruise control. Productive thinking using CPS requires extended effort. You need to keep at it, searching for possibilities that don't just pop into mind right away. Sometimes, for example, making deliberate efforts to stimulate ideas through all the senses can help you move beyond the obvious. Try looking at pictures, listening to music, sampling different odors, or even just going for a walk in the park. Doing some extra mental (or physical) exercise can pay off in fresh new insights and exciting possibilities.

4. *Seek combinations.* Very often, one possibility leads to another. You have probably observed many times, even in informal conversations, how one idea can lead to another. We often say, "Oh, yes … that reminds me of something else …" when someone says something that triggers a new thought in our own mind. In a CPS session, we try to make good use of that same experience, and so we encourage everyone in a group to be alert for new ways to connect one possibility to another. Some group leaders call this

"piggybacking," and we have always referred to it as "hitchhiking." By either name, the idea is the same: Look for ways to connect options and build new ones.

Guidelines for Focusing Options

What will you do after you have generated many, varied, and novel options? How will you examine and sort all those possibilities to reach a practical decision and locate those you want to use or develop further? As you begin to deal with these issues, your focus shifts from generating (and its related ground rules) to the complementary phase of focusing, and another important set of guidelines.

Unfortunately, some people seem to know only one way to analyze or evaluate options: with great and vigorous dispatch! It's as though, in driving their car, they only knew one way to stop—by slamming on the brakes, full force, screeching to a sudden and total stop. When it comes to possibilities, they say, "Well, I deferred judgment about as long as I possibly could. Now it's time to get rid of some of these dumb suggestions." They slam on the mental brakes as hard as they can. By finding fault with the options and limiting their view to a search for just one right answer or best solution, they often trap themselves into unproductive either/or thinking (we can only do it this way, or that way; it is possible, or it is impossible; an idea is great or it is useless), rather than looking for possible ways to look at possibilities carefully, constructively, and with an eye toward strengthening or developing those which are intriguing or promising. When it comes to new possibilities, as in so many other situations in life, it is often important and valuable to look at the shades of gray, and not just the white or black of them.

Sometimes, people become so negative in their approach that they can see only the weaknesses and limitations of every thought, dismissing the options one after another without any consideration of how they might be refined, strengthened, or developed to become successful. Too often, there's nothing left when they're finished. This is simply slaughtering ideas, and it is most often quite unproductive. To help overcome the numbing, possibility-crushing impact of a negative outlook, remember the following four basic ground rules for focusing.

1. *Practice affirmative judgment: Use a balanced approach that considers positives as well as negatives.* This does not mean accepting uncritically every option that has been generated. Instead, this principle emphasizes the need to screen, select, and then support your choices. Train yourself to look for the strengths or the positive aspects of options as the first part of your review. Begin by asking, "What are some things that appeal to me about the possibilities we've created?" Ask what's good about some of them, and try to find their advantages or strengths.

   Continue by considering their potentials—the "upstream" possibilities or future benefits that might emerge if some of your unusual options proved successful. Then, examine the limitations or concerns explicitly and thoroughly, but do so constructively. Consider what limitations might arise and how they might be dealt with, rather than just letting flow a steady stream of criticism. It helps to state your concerns in the form of a question ("How to …?" or "How might we …?") to keep the door open for ideas, rather than idea-killing statements ("We can't because …"). Affirmative Judgment should remind you, then, that evaluation and decision making are constructive processes intended to get the best out of our options, not just criticism. (There's a difference between critical and criticize.) Make a serious effort to seek a balanced assessment of the pluses, potentials, and concerns of the options. Examine your options thoroughly and rigorously, but emphasize constructive rather than destructive thinking. That is, put more emphasis on building possibilities up than on tearing them down.

2. *Be deliberate and explicit.* Effective focusing also involves making choices and decisions. It will be much easier, and usually less stressful, if you are deliberate and methodical in your approach. Think about the criteria that should influence your decision (which, for many decisions, may include formal, logical criteria, personal feelings, and values). Critical thinking is an important part of CPS applied effectively. The goal of a clear, detailed plan of action requires critical analysis as well as creative inspiration. Being deliberate means knowing and using specific tools or strategies to examine or analyze ideas, and being systematic in your approach.

   Being explicit about what you're doing is also important. Conflict or controversy in groups often arises when there are some hidden agendas or criteria that aren't known or shared by everyone. You can communicate, plan, and discuss options better when you work to be clear, honest, and specific about your criteria and methods for evaluating them—get things out in the open, so everyone can work together toward the best choices and decisions. Being explicit means expressing choices and reasons clearly, working hard to be aware of and to overcome hidden agendas, and using logic and good sense.

3. *Consider both novelty and appropriateness.* In selecting promising options (those you believe have interesting potential for successful application), be sure to consider both the novelty (is it a new or original possibility?) and the appropriateness (does it really move you forward or closer to a successful solution?) of the possibilities. New options that are not appropriate are unlikely to be put to use. Conversely, an appropriate possibility without novelty may not be sufficiently appealing or powerful to be carried into action.

4. *Stay on course.* Like any navigator, you need to keep your eyes on your destination, making decisions and correcting your course as you travel. You have to be sure to keep your eyes on your objectives, since, as one wit observed, "If you don't know where you're going, you might wind up somewhere else!"

Ask yourself, "What are the goals and objectives we're trying to achieve? Which of these options really help us to move in that direction?" Sometimes, the excitement and enthusiasm people experience in diverging leads them to lose sight of their initial purpose; all the options are fascinating for one reason or another. But, you must remind yourself to maintain your focus.

What is your vision? What will things look like if you are as successful as you can be? Are you getting options that lead you in that direction?

What is CPS?

So far, we have looked at the foundations or starting points for solving problems creatively: creative thinking or generating options, critical thinking or focusing options, and the basic principles and ground rules for Deferred and Affirmative Judgment. These are important principles for you to understand. But, in themselves, they are not enough to help you be an effective or productive problem solver. You will also need to be able to build on those foundations skillfully, by learning and using a deliberate process or system for creative problem solving—a well-organized, deliberate set of methods you can call upon whenever you need new ideas or solutions.

People have used many different methods to solve problems creatively, both formally and informally. Some involve guesswork or trial and error, which might lead to something new and useful if you're very fortunate. At the other extreme, some use very complicated, technical systems for decision analysis, which require a great deal of training and experience, and perhaps a powerful computer, to use. We use the phrase *creative problem solving* (without capital letters) to discuss any of these general efforts.

When we use CPS, or Creative Problem Solving with the capital letters, we are referring specifically to our approach and the growing community of practitioners in schools and other organizations worldwide. CPS is based on a substantial foundation of theory and research about creativity and problem solving—several decades of such scientific effort, in fact. Consult the bibliography at the end of the book if you're interested in the history and background or the details of that research and theory.

Most importantly, we believe that CPS is also a very practical, useful approach, suitable for the everyday situations that we all encounter. It comes from studying what people really need to do to solve problems creatively in the world in which we all have to operate, not just in the ideal or the special setting of the experimental laboratory. Everyone can use CPS, and using it will be helpful to you in your personal life, at home and in your family, and in your job or career.

Three Important Process Components and Six Specific Stages in CPS

During its history (more than four decades of research, development, and practical experience with groups), CPS has been a very dynamic model. It has grown and changed continuously in an on-going effort to represent as effectively as possible the strategies and actions used by effective, creative problem solvers in dealing with real problems and challenges. While CPS has been studied in experimental research, it has also always been a model that draws as closely as possible on what people really do when they're solving problems. It is not a laboratory model that is strange or uncomfortable in everyday life. To learn more about the history of CPS, you might read Isaksen, Treffinger, and Dorval (1997).

To understand the general structure of CPS, we might simply ask, "What are the most important things people have to be able to do when they're working on a problem?" We have found that efforts to solve problems creatively can be divided into three broad categories, which we call the three major process components of CPS. Within these three components, there are six specific stages during which creative and critical thinking abilities are used in harmony. Each stage involves a generating phase and a focusing phase.

Effective problem solvers do not always need all three components, or all six stages, and it is not necessary for them always to use the components or stages in a single, fixed (or "prescriptive") sequence or order. Instead, they begin by considering many important factors, and they choose deliberately the component(s) or stage(s) they need to be successful and productive in their thinking, whether they are working on their own or with a group. The transformation of CPS from a prescriptive, "lock step" series of stages or steps into a descriptive, flexible process framework has been one of the major outcomes of recent research and experience. This also led us to develop a "management component" to guide people in using CPS.

Keeping this flexibility of process in mind, consider Figures 1 and 2. Figure 1 seeks to represent graphically the flexibility of CPS as a descriptive process. Figure 2 presents a more detailed description of the stages in each component and the role of generating and focusing in each stage. Although Figure 2 may appear more "sequential," use Figure 1 to remind yourself that CPS need not be viewed (or applied) as a fixed or prescriptive stage model. (In Figure 2, *G* refers to "generate," and *F* refers to "focus.") The management component is also included in Figure 1.

In summary, then, the three major process components and the six specific stages of CPS can be described as follows:

Understanding the Challenge. You must be certain you are working on the right goals, challenges, or opportunities—asking the right question or stating the problem in a way that will help you find some productive answers. The three stages in this component are:

- *Constructing Opportunities:* Identifying and selecting a broad goal, challenge, or opportunity.
- *Exploring Data:* Exploring many aspects of the task and determining which aspect should be the principal focus for your CPS efforts.
- *Framing Problems*: Generating many possible problem statements and selecting or constructing a specific problem statement to use.

Generating Ideas. If you have clearly established the focus or direction for your CPS efforts, and you have a targeted or focused problem statement, you may need to generate ideas that have potential as solutions. There is just one stage in this component, which contains generating

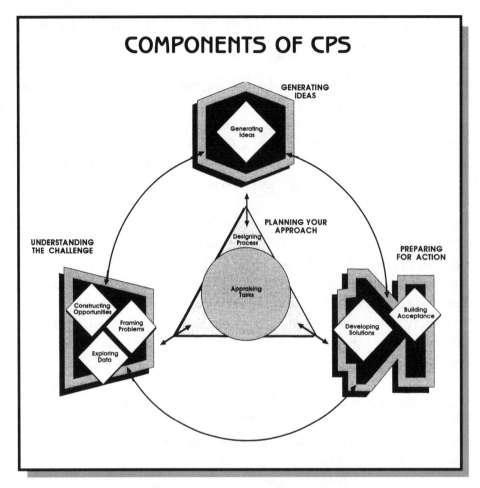

Figure 1: An Independent Components View of CPS
© S. G. Isaksen, K. B. Dorval, & D. J. Treffinger (2000). Used by permission.

many, new and unusual, or varied ideas to respond to the problem statement, then identifying the most promising possibilities.

Preparing for Action. If you have a number of new or promising options or possibilities, you may need to analyze, refine, or develop them into useful solutions and specific action steps. In this component, you will work on giving new and promising possibilities the best possible chance of becoming successful solutions or action plans. This component includes two stages, which are:

• *Developing Solutions*: Examining the most promising possibilities carefully and forming or shaping them into potential solutions.

• *Building Acceptance*: Exploring potential solutions and seeking support sources and ways to overcome resistance and increase the chances of successful implementation; then, developing a specific Action Plan, monitoring your actions, and revising them as necessary.

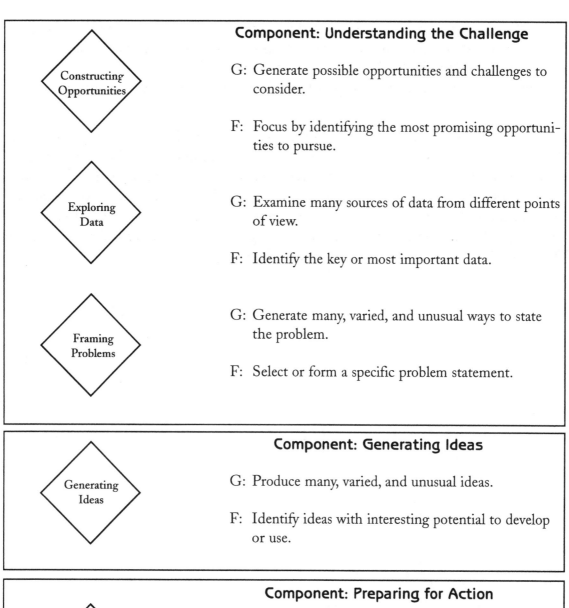

Component: Understanding the Challenge

Constructing Opportunities

G: Generate possible opportunities and challenges to consider.

F: Focus by identifying the most promising opportunities to pursue.

Exploring Data

G: Examine many sources of data from different points of view.

F: Identify the key or most important data.

Framing Problems

G: Generate many, varied, and unusual ways to state the problem.

F: Select or form a specific problem statement.

Component: Generating Ideas

Generating Ideas

G: Produce many, varied, and unusual ideas.

F: Identify ideas with interesting potential to develop or use.

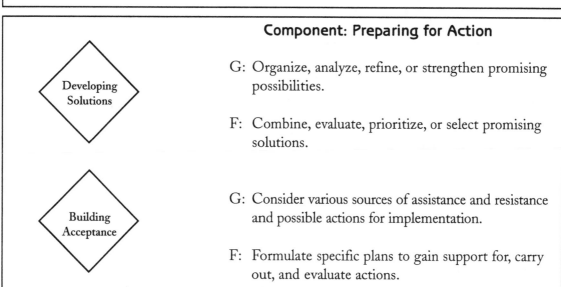

Component: Preparing for Action

Developing Solutions

G: Organize, analyze, refine, or strengthen promising possibilities.

F: Combine, evaluate, prioritize, or select promising solutions.

Building Acceptance

G: Consider various sources of assistance and resistance and possible actions for implementation.

F: Formulate specific plans to gain support for, carry out, and evaluate actions.

Figure 2: Three Major Process Components and Six Specific Stages of CPS

The Management Component, illustrated in Figure 1, is called "Planning Your Approach." It includes two stages, Appraising Tasks and Designing Process. These stages help individuals or groups to determine whether it is appropriate to use CPS for a certain task, and if so, how to determine the most effective ways to apply the CPS Process Components, stages, or tools.

Chapter 2 discusses preparing for CPS through the use of the Management Component. Then, chapters 3–5 discuss the three main process components. Chapter 3 examines Understanding the Challenge and the three specific stages it incorporates: Constructing Opportunities, Exploring Data, and Framing Problems. In chapter 4, you will learn about Generating Ideas. Chapter 5 presents the Preparing for Action component and explains the Developing Solutions and Building Acceptance stages. Finally, chapter 6 discusses applying CPS and presents some tips for using CPS successfully.

Chapter 2

Preparing for CPS

In preparing to use CPS, keep in mind that it is not an all-purpose process or panacea. There are many times, places, and situations for which CPS is well-suited—and others for which it is not. Therefore, since a contemporary approach to CPS should include tools to help you to determine when and how to use CPS effectively and appropriately, we developed a "management component" called Planning Your Approach.

Planning Your Approach includes two stages: Appraising Tasks and Designing Process. In this chapter, we will provide an overview of the Appraising Tasks stage, and we will also discuss several important factors to consider in Designing Process.

Appraising Tasks

A task is any job, piece of work, assignment, or activity that needs your attention, effort, and energy. It might have been given or assigned to you by someone else, something you initiated, or the by-product or combination of unique circumstances. Some tasks call for responses that are meaningful, novel, or original. The elements of the Appraising Tasks stage are summarized in Figure 3.

In Appraising Tasks, you have the opportunity to:

- identify and examine the key people involved in the task;
- identify the desired results or the outcomes you hope to attain or accomplish;
- explore the situation or context in which the task exists; and
- determine the appropriateness of using CPS on the task and the process options.

Identify and Consider the People

Identifying and examining the key players involved in a task is more than simply naming the people involved. It includes understanding how they are involved and their impact on the task. It also includes gathering information about such things as the nature of the clientship (responsibility for taking action) and how it will impact the task as well as the level of ownership among the individuals involved.

Identify Desired Results

Appraising Tasks provides the opportunity to explore the task and to identify the desired outcome or intended results. Clarifying the qualities of the desired outcome will help determine the appropriateness of CPS. For example, if there is no need for something new or different, then CPS may not be necessary. The level of importance of the outcome, and immediacy of the task (how soon you must act) are also factors that will influence your consideration of CPS.

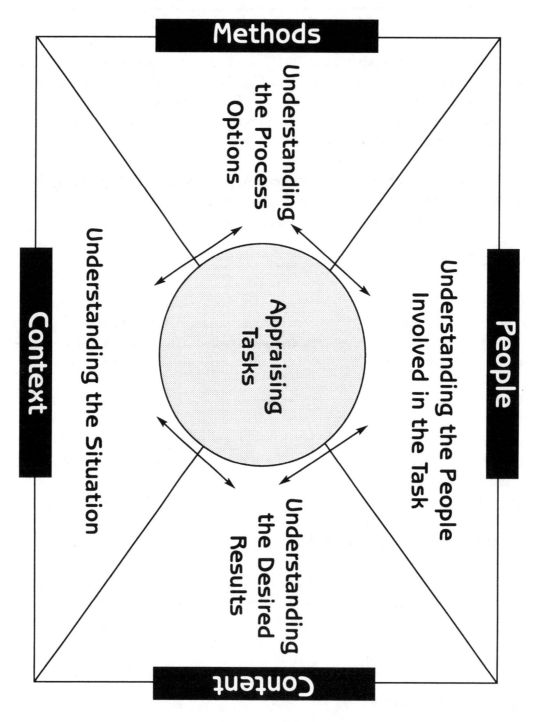

Figure 3: Appraising Tasks
© S. G. Isaksen, K. B. Dorval, & D. J. Treffinger (2000). Used by permission.

Examine the Context

The needs and general context in which the task is located will provide you with important information to consider before involving yourself in the task using CPS. Examining the context helps you understand the likelihood of action resulting from your CPS efforts. It also promotes understanding the opportunities that might exist for applying CPS.

Determine the Appropriateness of CPS

By understanding the people, the situation, and the desired outcome, you are in a better position to determine whether or not CPS is appropriate for the task. If you have the right people, who want a new and useful outcome, in a situation that calls for change, the situation may be appropriate for CPS. However, if the results of Appraising Tasks suggest that the right people are *not* involved, there is no desire for novelty, or the situation is not conducive to taking action, CPS may *not* be appropriate and other methodologies should be explored. These might include, for example, checking the available literature, using existing or previous solutions from history, conducting research or evaluation studies, or perhaps hiring a consultant. For different tasks, with different participants, and in varied settings, there may be many possible ways to seek the information, ideas, or directions you need.

Designing Process

Whenever you are working with CPS, you will be called on to be a productive thinker in a variety of different ways. You will need to be able to use your creative and critical thinking skills in relation to the content of the problem. That's the most obvious case. You will also need to be equally productive, effective, and efficient in several other ways. These are often described as the *executive* or *management* skills of CPS, or in more formal terms, the *metacognitive* skills. They have to do with how well you monitor and mange the process, throughout your efforts. You will need to develop an effective plan for applying CPS. Since CPS is a broad framework, you will need to tailor its use for the specific task through process planning. During your planning for CPS or the Designing Process stage of Planning Your Approach, you will:

- verify understanding of the language or vocabulary of CPS;
- confirm specific clientship and ownership;
- clarify the CPS roles if necessary (client, facilitator, and resource group member);
- locate a process starting point (e.g., a particular CPS component or stage); and
- prepare for applying CPS (individually or with a group, as appropriate).

Verify Understanding of the Language or Vocabulary of CPS

Skillful problem solvers should be able to describe or explain what they are doing, why they are doing it, and how. They should be comfortable with the vocabulary or terminology associated with the methods they use. Consider the analogy of going to the dentist. Would it inspire a great deal of confidence on your part, as you recline in the chair with your mouth open wide, to hear the dentist saying to an assistant, "I need the whatever-that-thing-is. You know, the long, pointy thing that holds the stuff we use so the patient won't feel any pain?" When the dentist uses the technical terms, even if you don't understand what they are, it suggests professionalism and competence. Familiarity with the language of one's field—the tools or strategies, the stages, the roles in CPS, for example—may seem to be jargon and, by itself, is certainly not enough to assure expertise. A common saying in the training field is that "you must be able to walk the walk, not just talk the talk." But a confident, comfortable level of expertise in CPS does involve knowing the language and being able to use it appropriately—walking the walk *and* talking the talk.

Confirm Specific Clientship

Although you may have examined the nature of clientship during Appraising Tasks, it may be helpful and necessary to confirm specifically the ownership of the task. Are there appropriate levels of interest, influence, and need for imagination? Will the results of your efforts have impact, and be able to make a difference? If ownership is not present or clear, consider modifying the task to establish or clarify ownership, or working with a different client (who has the needed interest, influence, and desire for new ideas or directions).

Clarify Roles for Applying CPS

When preparing to apply CPS, particularly in a group setting, it is important for all participants to understand their role and related responsibilities. For example, the client needs to know that, when applying CPS, the facilitator will not be contributing content suggestions or making decisions about content. The client needs to understand that he or she is primarily responsible for making content-related decisions and determining the direction and flow of the session's content. If CPS is applied using a resource group, its members need to be informed of their responsibilities for supporting the client during the session. Although resource group members need not be CPS experts, they do need to know enough about the task and the process to be helpful and productive.

Locate Your CPS Process Working Point

It is important in Designing Process to use the results of Appraising Tasks to determine where in the CPS framework to be working. Any of the three components or six stages might be an appropriate choice, depending upon your needs and the situation. Each stage can involve a variety of specific strategies or techniques you might need to use. You must be aware of the "tools" in your repertoire, and you must be able to make a variety of decisions about what to do, when and why to do it, and how to proceed. You may need to review your process or strategy choices several times when you are working on a complex challenge or situation. Appraising Tasks is not just a one time event, but an ongoing part of process management monitoring.

Selecting Strategies. Effective process management involves being able to plan strategies—to decide what tools to select and use, when, and for what reasons. Through experience in using CPS and regular debriefing of your efforts (see chapter 6), you will gain confidence in recognizing when certain methods or tools might be particularly appropriate or helpful to use. Some decisions will begin to be second nature to you, even though, at first, they may require very deliberate attention and effort. For example, as you gain experience with each component, you will know your choices better and you will recognize more quickly and easily where you wish or need to devote your efforts and activities.

Designing Process is also useful while you are engaged in CPS. Other decisions will always require you to make on-the-spot assessments and decisions. Is the group moving forward or going off on a tangent? How is the client reacting? Are the resource group members slowing down? Are all the ideas heading in the same direction? Does the group need help in stretching or broadening its viewpoint? And—for any of these questions—what might you do about it? What technique would be most appropriate to use? As you learn and practice a variety of tools for generating or analyzing ideas, you will also find that at other times, you may seek to apply a specific tool for a very particular purpose—to stimulate fluency, or originality of responses, or to help the group prioritize or evaluate ideas effectively.

As your experience and confidence grows with CPS and with many tools for each stage, you will probably feel more confident about experimenting—trying a certain tool at a time when you haven't ever used it before or modifying a tool to meet a certain situation's demands. One of the important differences between experts and novices, in CPS and many other areas, is that experts use their knowledge in creative, flexible ways, and are less concerned about "not doing it the right way." Novices are often much more literal, or more fearful of departing in the slightest way from the format or the way they were taught to use a particular tool. As your expertise and experience grows, you learn that the key question is not, "Am I doing this right?" but rather, "Are we moving forward toward a solution and a plan?"

With increasing experience and confidence in your own process knowledge and management, you should feel free to add new tools or varied techniques to your repertoire, from any model or approach. There is not just one right way to solve problems or to think creatively, and you should always feel free to incorporate appealing new ideas an strategies from any source.

Selecting Components. Although there are three components and six stages in the overall CPS framework, you will not always need or use all of them. Just because you own many tools does not mean you have to use all of them on every project. As Abraham Maslow, a well-known and respected psychologist, once observed, "If the only tool you have is a hammer, it's tempting to treat everything as if it were a nail."

Consider each situation, asking where you are, what you need, and where you would like to go. With these answers clearly in mind, you can examine each of the three CPS process components to determine which one (or more) will be most helpful.

If your need is to identify a future direction for change, to understand the current reality, or to identify pathways to move an existing situation in new directions, then the Understanding the Challenge component is an appropriate starting point. You may have only a general goal or concern in mind, and you have not yet begun to examine what's involved in it or to formulate a specific statement of the problem.

If you need to gather ideas for solving a specific problem, then the Generating Ideas component may be most appropriate. You have already looked at a great deal of data about your situation, and the opportunity or challenge is quite well-defined, so that you already have an open-ended problem statement (in the "How might I ...?" or "In What Ways Might [IWWM] ...?" form, for example). If you discover that the ideas you generate are not really moving in any new or productive directions, or that you've missed some key data, these might be warning signs to revisit one or more of the stages in Understanding the Challenge. It is always possible, as necessary, to move freely among any of the components or stages.

If you need to make decisions about options, to strengthen promising alternatives, or to develop an effective implementation plan, the Preparing for Action component may be your most appropriate starting point. You may already have a number of new and intriguing ideas for a specific problem or challenge, and you will need to plan for success. You will enhance your likelihood of success by working deliberately on Developing Solutions and Building Acceptance.

Should you choose to work with all of the components, consider whether each component or stage will require the same degree of time and energy. You might allocate more time to one component that is your primary concern, and less (or even none) to the other components. You might also decide to manage your time by working on only one component in a single session, extending your work over a longer period of time. The most important point to remember is that it is certainly *not* necessary that CPS always involve using every component, all six stages, or completing all your work in a prescribed sequence of steps or stages or in a single session. These are all decisions that you will need to make deliberately (and monitor continuously) as you apply CPS in different situations.

Chapter 3
Understanding the Challenge

"The only exercise some minds get is jumping to conclusions!"
—Pansy Torrance

Many people are in so much of a hurry to solve their problem that they don't pay enough attention to deciding just what the problem really is. Sometimes everything works out satisfactorily anyway, thanks to plenty of hard work—and more than a little good fortune. Often, however, after hours (or once in awhile, days, or even months!) of work that doesn't seem to be accomplishing anything, they finally realize they have been asking the wrong questions or working on the wrong problem. Some problem-solving researchers have emphasized the need to look closely at the way problems are defined, framed, or constructed before the process of solving them can even begin. Researchers have even proposed that the process of problem finding should be treated as an entirely independent or separate area, distinct from problem solving. We agree that the early work of understanding and structuring the problem is very important. But we believe that there are really several aspects to this task:

- before working with any CPS components or stages, prepare for CPS and determine its appropriateness for your situation and goals (Appraising Tasks, from chapter 2) and decide where in the CPS framework to begin your work (Designing Process, also from chapter 2); and

- apply appropriate strategies and use tools for Understanding the Challenge if you have decided that you need to clarify your situation or task and frame it in constructive ways that will stimulate new directions.

Using the CPS Understanding the Challenge component will be rewarding and productive when you need to be sure you're formulating or shaping an opportunity or challenge in the best possible way. If you need focus or direction for your CPS efforts, applying one or more of the three stages of Understanding the Challenge will make it easier for you to use your imagination, creativity, judgment, and critical thinking in productive ways as you continue your efforts.

Understanding the Challenge involves such questions and issues as, "What are we working on?" "What are our goals and challenges?" "What are the important data we need to consider?" "How will we [identify … formulate … develop … recognize … construct … tackle] the problem as we work together?" "What is the best way to pose the problem we really want to solve?" As you work in this component, you must be able and willing to apply the basic ground rules or guidelines for deferred and affirmative judgment, and to use both divergent and convergent thinking in harmony to generate and focus options.

When you are dealing with a situation that requires clarification, focus, and definition, there are several important benefits of using tools from the Understanding the Challenge component and some genuine risks in failing to do so. These are summarized in Table 2.

Each of the three CPS stages in Understanding the Challenge serves a unique purpose, the importance and usefulness of which you will need to consider as you work on the problem. Constructing Opportunities helps you identify a broad, general goal or need within an unclear or fuzzy situation or challenge and formulate it in a constructive way. Exploring Data helps you draw out important factors in understanding where you are now and where you really hope to be heading; it helps you find the essential elements or the "heart" of a mess. Framing Problems guides you in constructing a very specific and focused or targeted question to use for generating and analyzing new ideas.

Benefits of Understanding the Challenge	Risks of *Not* Understanding the Challenge
1. Setting a focus or direction for your subsequent CPS efforts.	1. Getting lots of ideas that don't really matter to anyone or anything.
2. Identifying the key concerns for which you really want and need new ideas.	2. Getting ideas that may fail because critical issues or data were disregarded or overlooked at the beginning.
3. Spurring the imagination and heightening innovation and creative process.	3. Being unable to generate productive ideas because the question is poorly worded.
4. Capturing the curiosity, energy, and motivation of the group.	4. Getting only the same old ideas because you're using the same old ways of defining the problem.

Table 2: Benefits or Risks of Attending (or not) to
Understanding the Challenge Component

Constructing Opportunities

Constructing Opportunities is an appropriate stage of CPS to apply when you are beginning with only a very broad, general task or challenge that needs clarity and direction before you can proceed.

Through Appraising Tasks, you've established a general domain to work on, whereas in Constructing Opportunities, you're exploring that domain to locate and clarify the most important opportunities or challenges within it. Constructing Opportunities helps you "map out" the very broad domain and deal with the primary question, "What is the challenge, opportunity, or concern on which we are going to be working?" An opportunity for CPS might be a situation, goal, challenge, or concern that is broad, general, and still not precisely defined or constructed.

There may well be many different areas of opportunity in any task or domain of concern to you, and perhaps several of them will need your attention at one time or another. But, you can't really work on all of them at the same time. What are the opportunities that need attention and effort in your life? And how can you decide which ones to work on first, and which ones to set aside for another time?

If you begin with a task that you are able to express only in a very global, imprecise, or ill-defined way, it might include a rather large number of opportunities on which you might concentrate. For example, if your task involves wanting to move your personal life or career in new directions, several plausible opportunities might include:

- increasing my income;
- choosing a new career direction;
- planning for retirement;
- enhancing productivity; or
- making my work more exciting.

A statement of an opportunity is not a problem statement; it is a broad challenge or situation on which you want or need to work. None of these statements offers a specific, precise, or detailed description of a problem to work on. To attempt to solve any one of them in their present form would probably lead to a "buckshot" approach, with ideas flying willy-nilly in every direction. If your problem statement lacks direction, it may be easy to waste time and energy in brainstorming that appears haphazard or dissatisfying. They might well be reasonable messes to explore.

Your efforts in Constructing Opportunities will help you untangle complicated situations so you can direct your problem-solving efforts where you really want them. Real problems rarely come our way in a clear, neatly stated, precise form. Time and energy must be spent getting them ready to solve.

Generating When Constructing Opportunities

As you have already read in chapter 1, CPS involves both generating and focusing options. So, in Constructing Opportunities, as in all six CPS stages, you will engage in both generating and focusing. Generating in Constructing Opportunities, which is what some people refer to as "being sensitive to problems," has to do with finding out what might be some possible starting points for problem solving, or recognizing some of the opportunities that are around and about in any situation, task, or challenge.

The Three Bs for Opportunities. To help you identify possible goals or directions for your CPS efforts, keep in mind the three Bs of Constructing Opportunities:

- *Broad.* Keep your opportunity statements broad so you don't prematurely limit your thinking. If you try to focus them too much or too soon, you might miss the most important opportunity to be creative. In a career opportunity, for example, limiting yourself by saying, "I want to find a job with a new employer" might prevent you from thinking about improving or modifying an existing job or creating a career of your own.

- *Brief.* Limit the number of words. Express the opportunity in "headline" form to keep it clear and simple. If you say, "I want to increase my income by at least 25% without having to work on holidays or weekends and without having to take any new courses or examinations, while building specifically on my bagpipe-playing hobby," you might feel confused and lost before you start. Instead, you might just say, "I'd like to use my hobby to increase my income."

- *Beneficial.* Always try to word your opportunity in a positive or affirmative manner. Focus on what you do want to move toward, not what you don't want. This will help you establish and maintain a sense of progress or forward motion. For example, instead of saying, "I'm feeling lousy because I'm in poor shape," it would be much better to say, "I want to improve my health and fitness."

WIBAI and WIBNI. It is very common for people to think of a problem as something that's wrong, that needs correcting or fixing-up, and as something unpleasant, stressful, and worrisome. These kinds of tasks are "WIBAIs," which stands for "Wouldn't It Be Awful If ...." It is true that problems often do appear this way. On the other hand, it can be helpful to learn to look for the WIBNIs, too. These are the "Wouldn't It Be Nice If ..." situations, which are sometimes described as opportunities, wishes, aspirations, hopes, dreams, or great chances. These can also be productive starting points for CPS. Often, when you start with a WIBAI, it will help you gain confidence, enthusiasm, and direction if you look for ways to turn it around and make it into a WIBNI. For example, if you begin with a negative task statement such as, "I am really feeling lousy and out of shape," try redirecting to a more positive statement such as, "Wouldn't it be nice if I could get into better condition and feel healthier?" When you are generating in Constructing Opportunities, try writing several headlines that start with WIBAI ... or WIBNI ..., and then try turning the WIBAIs into more WIBNIs.

Some Positive Opportunity Starters. Another way to express constructive opportunity statements is to remind yourself to use action verbs such as:

improve	extend	enhance	develop
establish	support	promote	produce
invent	design	encourage	change
increase	expand	stimulate	build

Through years of working with CPS, we have found many questions to help identify worthwhile and challenging opportunity statements. The questions in Table 3 were adapted from several previous lists (e.g., Isaksen and Treffinger, 1985; Parnes, Noller, & Biondi, 1977).

For this opportunity or challenge ...

1. What would you like to do, have, or accomplish?
2. What would you like to be able to do better or differently?
3. For what do you wish you had more resources?
4. What more would you like to accomplish? What outcomes would be inspiring?
5. What makes you angry, tense, or frustrated about it?
6. What makes you really excited or happy about it?
7. What have you complained about, and how could it be improved or resolved?
8. If you had one wish in this area, for what would you ask?
9. What would you like to stimulate others to do?
10. What takes too long? What would help it move faster?
11. What waste or limits might be changed or eliminated?
12. What would really help you move forward with something important?
13. What would increase your motivation and enthusiasm?
14. What are the best emerging opportunities of which you want to be sure to take advantage?

Table 3: Constructing Opportunities: Questions

Focusing When Constructing Opportunities

When you are considering which opportunity to choose for your CPS efforts, you will need to consider the important concern of ownership. There are three important concerns in establishing ownership:

- *Influence*. Can you take action? Is the task one for which you have the responsibility and the opportunity to do something?

- *Interest*. Do you care? Do you really want to take action about the task?

- *Imagination*. Do you really need new or better possibilities than those that already exist for dealing with the task? Do you really need to invest your creative energy?

In addition, you must also apply several criteria as you sift and sort possible opportunities. These sorting criteria include:

- *Importance*. Is it really important for you to work on this particular task? Does it have consequences that are critical in nature for you or others?

- *Priority.* Is it a task on which timely action is especially important? Is now the best or most appropriate time to tackle it?

- *Stability or change.* If you do not work on this task now, what will happen? Will the situation deteriorate or become worse? Might it become much more difficult to work on at a future time?

Generating

- What's important about this opportunity or challenge?
- What do I (we) find interesting?
- About what am I (we) concerned?
- What would I like to do better or differently in this area?
- What's nagging at me about this situation?
- What about this situation demands my (our) attention?
- What new opportunities are there in this situation?
- About what in this situation am I really excited?
- About what paradoxes and puzzles am I wondering?

Focusing

- What demands are really most pressing?
- What am I (we) most prepared to work on now?
- What concerns are most pressing or important?
- What will happen if I (we) don't deal with these?
- What risks are worth it? What risks are necessary?
- What are my (our) priorities?
- What do I (we) most hope to preserve, achieve, or attain?
- What do I (we) most want to expand, enhance, or improve?
- What are my (our) "bottom line" goals and concerns?

Table 4: Some Key Questions for Constructing Opportunities

Use the criteria for ownership and these sorting criteria to help you decide which opportunity, among the many you have before you, represents the best choice on which to work at the present time. When you have completed Constructing Opportunities, you will need to do additional work on Designing Process. You may choose to look more closely at the opportunity, working in the Exploring Data stage, or you may decide that you are ready to consider another stage or component.

Summary

Table 4 presents a number of key questions about Constructing Opportunities. These are not a pilot's preflight checklist in which you must ask each question in the correct order on every occasion. Rather, they will illustrate for you, and remind you about, the important aspects of Constructing Opportunities. We will present a similar list of questions to summarize each of the six CPS process stages throughout the book. Remember, too, that they might be questions for an individual (I/me) or a group (we/us), depending on who the client is or the nature of the ownership in the situation.

Exploring Data

The Exploring Data stage in Understanding the Challenge helps you locate and define the important clusters within a task or situation and sharpen or refine the focus for your CPS efforts. It involves asking, "What part of this situation is really most important to focus on?" Exploring Data is important for several reasons. It helps you to:

1. break away from stereotyped or habit-bound thinking about the opportunity, challenge, or situation;
2. look broadly at a task so you aren't held back by important considerations that were overlooked;
3. sort out just what you really do and don't know about a situation, avoiding premature closure;
4. set priorities—locate the parts of a situation that stand out and really demand some attention and action; and
5. unlock previously hidden patterns or interrelationships among data in an opportunity or challenge.

Suppose, for example, you were working on a broad opportunity statement such as, "WIBNI … our training programs were more exciting and effective." Exploring Data might help you discover several major clusters of concern, such as: using modern training technology and resources; increasing staff members' motivation; and building staff members' ownership in the training programs. Each one might lead you to view or approach the opportunity in a different or unique way. If you decided that lack of ownership and involvement of trainees in the planning was the real heart of the matter, ideas for using more technology might not have been very helpful.

If you had simply attempted to "solve the training problem" without looking more closely, you might have come up with some productive ideas. But, the chances are high that you might instead have become hopelessly and unproductively entangled. The result might have been a jumble of ideas that seemed to go in so many different directions that you wouldn't really know what might be done with any of them. The purpose of Exploring Data, therefore, might be summarized as helping you determine what part of your task most needs your CPS efforts.

When Exploring Data, you will be examining a task situation from different viewpoints, and gathering information, impressions, perceptions, and feelings about it. Then, you will determine

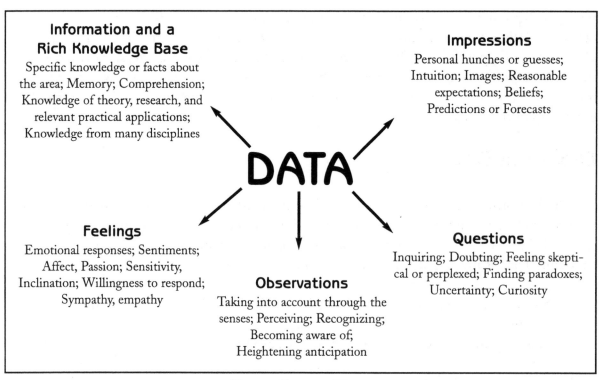

Information and a Rich Knowledge Base
Specific knowledge or facts about the area; Memory; Comprehension; Knowledge of theory, research, and relevant practical applications; Knowledge from many disciplines

Impressions
Personal hunches or guesses; Intuition; Images; Reasonable expectations; Beliefs; Predictions or Forecasts

DATA

Feelings
Emotional responses; Sentiments; Affect, Passion; Sensitivity, Inclination; Willingness to respond; Sympathy, empathy

Observations
Taking into account through the senses; Perceiving; Recognizing; Becoming aware of; Heightening anticipation

Questions
Inquiring; Doubting; Feeling skeptical or perplexed; Finding paradoxes; Uncertainty; Curiosity

Figure 4: Sources of Data

which data seem most important to gain a more specific focus or direction for Understanding the Challenge. Exploring Data helps you attain a sharp, focused understanding of the task and situation.

An obvious, but humorous, example of the need for Exploring Data has been used as a comedy sketch by many entertainers. A person is preparing to watch television, but when the set is turned on, nothing happens. After fiddling with the power switch and a few other knobs and dials, banging on the front and sides of the set, and showing various other signs of frustration, a repair company is summoned to the scene. Alas, it is embarrassing, frustrating, and needlessly expensive when the repair person points out to the customer that the power cord for the set wasn't plugged into the electrical outlet! (Technical support personnel of many computer manufacturers tell much the same story.)

Every task and the situation surrounding it contains a vast array of information or data. In most situations, there will be considerably more data available than you will usually be able to recognize or use. Some of these data are not really very important. For example, if you're thinking about how to organize the items on your desk top, the observation that the room has a brown carpet might be a valid piece of data—but it is one that is most likely irrelevant. The weather outside would also not be too important—but it would be much more pertinent if you were deciding whether or not to go to the beach. In Exploring Data, then, your task is to seek as much and as varied data as possible that will be important for you to consider in determining what needs your attention.

Generating When Exploring Data

Generating when Exploring Data involves conducting an open-ended search for many possibilities. Look at your task in many different ways. Look for any insights that will help you understand it better. Your goal is to avoid missing or ignoring important data. Finding the "unexpected but important" element in a task results from a thorough job of generating when Exploring Data. Several kinds of data are important. It is important to look beyond the clear facts and obvious information that jumps out at you right away. Often, the heart of the challenge will be found in what you're uncertain, puzzled, perplexed, or confused about. Your work on Exploring Data should take into account:

Who?	What?	When?
• Who's involved? • Who has created or added to the situation? • Who will have to help deal with it? • Who's concerned about the task, or excited about it?	• What has been done before? • What resources do we have or need? • What would we like to see happen? • What if we had a magic wand?	• When did I become aware of this? • When do I think most about it? • When must action be taken? • When is the best or worst time to work on it?
Where?	**Why?**	**How?**
• Where does the action take place? • Where else has anyone dealt with a similar situation? • Where are the best or worst places to be? • Where would we like to be with this task in the near future?	• Why do we have this situation? • Why hasn't it been dealt with? What's holding us back? • Why do we really want to deal with it? • Why might anyone not want to deal with this situation?	• How do I see this situation? • How do others view it? • How would we like to see changes made? • How would our ideal be different from the present? • How have other efforts succeeded or failed?

Table 5: Sample Questions for the 5 Ws and H

Information and a Rich Knowledge Base. Knowledge of specific events, people, places, or situations; news; what is known and can be perceived, calculated, verified, discovered, concluded, or inferred; the information you can remember and use.

Impressions. Images from your past experiences or beliefs; your hunches, notions, or intuitive perceptions or thoughts; what your "sixth sense" tells you about the situation.

Observations. What you notice, see, hear, touch, taste, or feel—looking carefully at the mess from many vantage points and recording information you receive through the senses.

Feelings. Your awareness of or sensitivity to emotional responses, sentiments, or affective responses; your concerns for harmony and relationships; the impact of situations on people.

Questions. The areas about which you feel uncertain, confused, or unclear; aspects of the situation for which you lack information; your curiosity, the paradoxes, or the feeling of perplexity about the situation. Figure 4 illustrates some of these key elements in Exploring Data.

Think of a task or challenge, in one way, as a diamond in the rough. It might have great merit and value, but until it has been skillfully cut and polished, that value cannot be realized. The expert diamond cutter examines the stone patiently, measuring, weighing, looking from every angle, preparing it for the precise break that will unlock the gem's brilliance and beauty. In Exploring Data, you will examine the task from many different perspectives, too, looking for the data that will unlock the most productive insights and understanding of your task and situation.

Two tools are particularly helpful during the generating phase of Exploring Data.

1. *Use the 5 Ws and an H.* Probe the task by asking many questions about it. The six questions you probably learned in school will serve you very well: *Who? What? When? Where? Why?* and *How?* For example, asking *Who?* will help you identify the key people in your mess. Asking *What?* helps to bring out important data about the things—materials, resources, actions, challenges, or concerns that are important. Each of the six questions can be used to help you explore your situation as you ask, "What is it about this situation that keeps it on my mind? Where is the real heart of the problem or challenge?" Some sample questions for each of the six words are listed in Table 5. Use them to help you dig deeply into your task and search beyond the obvious information at the surface of it. (The terms I and we can be interchanged in any of these questions.)

2. *Compare your "Desired Future State" with your "Current Reality."* Figure 5 will help you do this. Your Current Reality involves the data about the way things are now. Your Desired Future State expresses the situation as it will be when you have solved the problem. The challenge, of course, is to move from here to there. By listing important elements for each, you can begin to search for common themes or patterns—the essential concerns in your task.

Focusing When Exploring Data

After generating or considering many sources of data about your mess, you will need next to focus your thinking. Any situation involves a number of different parts or pieces; your efforts might be directed or channeled toward one part of the concern or another. If you did not pause for focusing when Exploring Data, and instead tried to "take everything along with you," the chances are high that you will soon be overrun with information. It is possible to have so much information that you can't do anything useful with any of it.

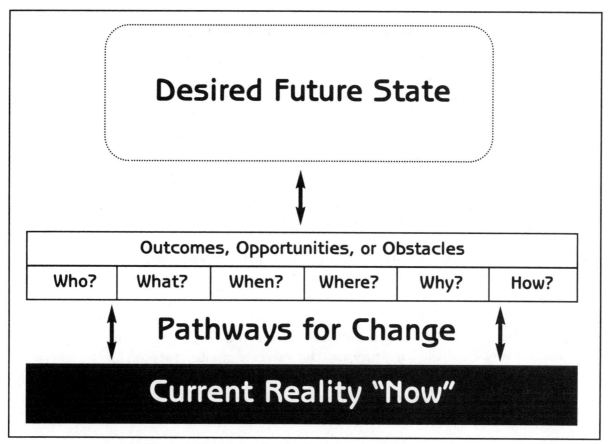

Figure 5: Comparing Current Realities with Desired Futures

Focusing is an important phase of your work in Exploring Data (just as it is in any CPS stage). It involves examining your data carefully to determine the central or primary opportunity or concern. Focusing when Exploring Data helps you find the part of the task on which you will want to focus or concentrate your efforts. The following questions use several different words or phrases to illustrate the task of focusing when Exploring Data; one or another of these might give you a sharp, clear understanding of the purpose:

- What's really making this situation a challenge or an opportunity?
- What's the heart of the situation?
- What's the essence—the most critical area of concern or opportunity?
- What's the central issue in this situation?

Several specific tools will help you during the focusing phase of Exploring Data. These include:

1. *Locating hits and hot spots.* Your first step in focusing is looking back at your list of data and marking any and all of the items that are hits for you. What's a hit? Check the key words in Table 6.

An idea may be a "hit" for you for any of these reasons ...

- On target
- Relevant
- Exciting
- Clear
- Intriguing
- Workable
- Right "on the money"

- Feels right
- Interesting
- Moves forward
- "Sparkles"
- Fascinating
- Solves problem
- Goes in right direction

Table 6: What's a Hit?

When you are identifying the hits in your list of data, just ask yourself, "Which pieces of data really tell the most about the task and what we need to work on within that task?"

After you have marked the hits, examine them closely to determine where the "hot spots" are located and what they are. Hot spots are groups of several hits (two or more) that all address or deal with a common theme, issue, or important dimension of the mess. They are the threads or strands that run through the task and very likely reveal the part of the task that is its greatest opportunity, challenge, or concern for you.

As you generated the list of data, there may have been several key issues that keep coming up repeatedly in different ways. You might or might not have been aware of these areas, and seeking the hot spots in the data can help you recognize them and test which ones best describe the most important or essential part of your concern for that mess.

The hot spots are significant clusters within the data. Identifying them helps you understand the situation and make it more manageable; it also guides you in finding greater clarity, focus, and direction for other CPS activities.

2. *Use focusing stems for clarity.* As you look at the data, it can be helpful in converging to pose some questions or make some summary statements that begin with, "If I had a magic wand ...," "What I really wish or hope is ...," or "The direction I'd really like to see our search take is ...." These phrases often help you cut away extraneous or minor bits of data and look more closely at what really needs to be solved.

3. *Paraphrase key data relationships.* When you look at several items of data that form a hot spot, it can be helpful to examine that cluster and ask yourself, "How are these items all

related to each other? What do they have in common?" After defining the common relationship, paraphrase it. Express the common theme concisely and in your own words to name the cluster.

These focusing tools in Exploring Data will help you locate the most important and promising part of your task. You can then use your process-planning skills to assess your next steps. You may decide to take your key data forward to the Framing Problems stage of Understanding the Challenge, or you might decide that another stage or component can be more helpful. If you decide later that some of the other data or clusters might really be more important than you thought at first, you can easily return to any of them whenever you need or want to do so.

Generating

- What information do I have? Would I like? Do I need?
- What information sources should be checked?
- Who else is involved? To whom should I talk?
- What might I touch, taste, observe, feel, explore?
- What have I overlooked? What else?
- What feelings, hunches, impressions, ideas, questions, or observations might be involved?
- What has already been tried? With what results?
- When am I concerned? When is it on my mind? Where?
- What is preventing me from doing what I want/need to do?
- Why haven't I already solved this problem or done what I want to do?
- Why is this a concern or interest to me?
- Has anyone else addressed this?
- How might I find out more?

Focusing

- What data are most important to consider?
- Which parts of the data might be grouped together?
- What clusters or hot spots best describe the most important themes or priorities?
- What strands or issues run through all these data?
- What's the real "essence" of your task and situation?
- What patterns do I see in these data?
- What concerns or opportunities must be addressed first?
- What additional data might be gathered before we proceed?

Table 7: Some Key Questions for Exploring Data

Summary

When Exploring Data, your generating and focusing efforts help you explore the situation and find the most important or central concern on which you want to focus and direct your CPS efforts. Some of the Key Questions for Exploring Data are presented in Table 7. Again, keep in mind that the questions can be stated in the singular or plural form for an individual or group problem.

Framing Problems

The Framing Problems stage of Understanding the Challenge is used to help you define a specific or focused problem statement. Framing Problems involves defining a workable, stimulating, and specifically worded problem statement.

To follow once again the training example presented earlier in this chapter, suppose you determined that the people in your training programs just don't seem to care much about being there. "It would really be great," you might say, "if we could make them feel a sense of motivation and ownership." This focus for your task will help you in shaping your approach to Framing Problems. Just a few of the specific problem statements it might lead you to consider, for example, include:

- How might we increase staff ownership of training programs?
- How might we expand staff input in planning training programs?
- How might we enhance our assessment of staff members' perceived needs?
- In what ways might we build motivation for training?

These statements would be likely to provide a productive foundation or direction for your search for new ideas or solutions. They provide many ways of identifying a very specific question to explore in detail. Your problem statement focuses on the heart of your task, expressing your challenge in a way that invites you to search for many possibilities and options.

What Makes a Good Problem Statement?

In order to recognize a good problem statement, it might be helpful to look at some that are not very good. Like most people, you have probably sat in many groups or committees and heard such common statements as: "The problem is … we don't have enough money (or time) to do the job; … we don't have the support we need; … nobody appreciates all the hard work we do," or, "We can't do this because … it's never been done this way before; … the old, tried-and-true ways are good enough; … we need to have a task force study it first; or, … the union will object (or management will object) …" and so on.

What's wrong with these problem statements? First, they are all negative. Most people report that these kinds of discussions are depressing, discouraging, or self-defeating before anyone even tries to do anything. Second, they turn thinking off, rather than turning it on. These statements tend to give people more reasons not to act than to try to do anything. They have a kind of built-in suggestion that says, "Nothing's going to work, so why bother trying?"

What we would prefer, then, is a problem statement that is positive or constructive, and that invites or turns on good thinking. To accomplish this, we have found that a good problem statement should meet several important criteria. These are:

- *Question form.* In a way, "problem statement" is a misnomer, since a good problem poses a question rather than making a statement.

- *Invites ideas.* A good problem statement invites you to generate many (and richer) ideas. It draws you naturally into the flow of creative thinking.

- *Free of limiting criteria.* A good problem statement should not box you in or limit your thinking by being filled with limitations, restrictions, qualifications, or criteria. It is worded as broadly and openly as possible so many ideas—including some that might be quite different and unusual—can be produced.

- *Concisely stated.* A good problem statement should be brief and to the point so it will be easily understood and readily used as a starting point for generating ideas.

Three Elements of a Good Problem Statement

With the indicators of a good problem statement in mind, there are three basic elements to remember:

1. *Invitational stem.* The problem statement begins with a phrase that invites group members to be creative thinkers. We have found three such invitational stems to be particularly useful and helpful:

    - IWWM ... ⟷ In What Ways Might ...
    - HM ... ⟷ How Might ...
    - H2 ... ⟷ How To ...

2. *Clearly stated ownership.* The problem statement should also express clearly on whose problem you're working. This ownership clarification is usually linked closely to the invitational stem. For example: IWWMI ... represents, "In What Ways Might I ...," in which it is clear that you're working on a problem for which one person ("I," the client in the session) has ownership and responsibility. IWWMW, which represents, "In What Ways Might We ..." implies group ownership or clientship. Often, the stem will be accompanied by a specific name, such as "IWWM John," in which case you know that it is John's problem on which you are being asked to work.

3. *Verb and objective.* The problem statement should make clear the action and objective for the question. For example, a problem statement might be, "In what ways might we increase membership in our group?" The verb *increase* is constructive and active; the objective *membership [in our group]* states clearly and concisely that we want to find ideas to increase. Several illustrations of problem statements from CPS groups are presented below:

- IWWMI increase students' motivation in the classroom?
- H2 prioritize my use of work time?
- IWWMW create and maintain productive staff teams?
- H2 create a vision for our team or group?
- IWWMW move projects ahead?
- H2 increase our productivity?
- HMI develop or enhance my own creativity?
- HMW make staff meetings more productive?
- HMW remove [sex, age, race, ethnic] bias from our work group?
- H2 enhance collaboration in working groups?
- H2 make more time for developing new ideas or projects?
- HMW promote harmony and collaboration?
- IWWMW increase chances of success for all students?
- H2 help our people expand their interest in improving their creative and critical thinking?

Generating When Framing Problems

Generating when Framing Problems begins by posing many IWWM ..., HM ..., or H2 ... questions. Look for a number of different possibilities and for alternate ways of expressing any of the questions. What are some questions that would really do a good job of stating the problem?

You are not seeking "answers" or solutions to any questions. Instead, you are trying to find the best, most powerful, or most appealing way to ask the question. You are exploring many possible ways to express the question that you really want to ask. Be sure to look for a good, full set of possibilities. We have often found that some of the most interesting and useful ways of stating the problem emerge in the second half of a list of as many as 30 to 40 possibilities.

Dancing With Words. It is often helpful to take one of your problem statements and use it as a starting point to consider many other possible wordings in a playful, exploratory way; we call this, "Dancing With Words."

1. Write down the first statement. For example, it might be, "In what ways might I attract new customers?"

2. Underline or circle the verb (attract) and, under it, list many other verbs that might be used instead. Write down as many verbs as come to mind—perhaps a dozen other possibilities.

3. Underline or circle the objective (new customers) and do the same thing.

Your results might look like this example:

IWWMI	Attract	New customers
	locate	business
	find	more buyers
	entice	sales
	insure	repeat purchases
	guarantee	different ages
	drag in	big spenders
	catch	broader sales base
	capture	risk takers
	win	new faces
	earn	members
	excite	group sales
	create	sales by referrals

4. Test several new problem statements by "mixing and matching" any of the verbs with any of the objectives. Some might seem very similar to your original question. However, others might offer a new choice that appeals to you because a certain word or phrase seems to work better or seems more appropriate than the original. Sometimes, you will also discover an added benefit, as occasionally one of the new combinations opens up an entirely new direction for the problem that hadn't occurred to you previously.

Asking "Why?" and "Why Else?" Another tool to help you when generating in Framing Problems is to use the "why" or "why else" questions. These tools can help you locate a broader redefinition of the problem if you have allowed your original view to become too narrow. For example, consider a theater group who posed the problem, "IWWMW sell more tickets?"

We asked, "Why do you want to sell more tickets?," and they replied, "To get more people into the auditorium for each performance." A broader problem statement then emerged: "HMW get more people to attend each performance?"

Asking "Why else do you want to sell more tickets?" led to the answer, "To increase our earned revenue." That suggested another possible problem statement, also broader than the original version: "How might we expand the theater's earned revenues?"

Focusing When Framing Problems

One of the most important decisions you will make in any CPS session involves your choice of a problem statement; the course and direction for all the subsequent stages will be influenced by this decision. How should you proceed?

Keep in mind one major question: "Which problem statement does the best job of posing the question for which I really need and want new ideas?" This will help you be as productive as possible when focusing in the Framing Problems stage.

The Head and Shoulders Test. Firestien and Treffinger (1983) proposed the head and shoulders test as a probable first step in focusing on a problem statement. This test simply involves asking, "Does one of the problem statements I have listed stand head and shoulders above all the rest?" If so, it should be strongly considered as your choice.

Is it open-ended or rich in potential for generating many ideas? Is it free of limiting constraints or criteria? And, above all else, does it express the problem in a way that you are certain is accurate and complete? Does it really get to the heart of the issue?

Hits and Hot Spots. Upon occasion, one compelling, head and shoulders standout problem statement does emerge. We have found that, much more commonly, there will be several interesting possibilities among 30 or 40 in your list. Under these circumstances, you can use the same "hits and hot spots" tools that were described in the Exploring Data section of this chapter.

If you identify a number of hits in your list of problem statements, you can search for a hot spot or common theme among them, or you might want to compare them with each other to explore whether one is more intriguing and powerful than the others. It is often possible to merge several interesting problem statements into one, choosing a verb from one and the wording of an objective from another.

Be careful, however, about not simply linking or stringing several objectives together into one complex problem statement. If you combine more than one key objective into a single problem statement, your efforts later may be easily fragmented and confusing. Combine several problem statements into one, then, when they all fit together comfortably in relation to a common overall objective or direction. For example, in the theater example, combining the problem statements, "IWWMW increase season subscribers?" and "HMW attract more program advertising revenue?" might not fit together very well. The group might drift or wander between one question or the other when Generating Ideas, without real clarity about what kinds of ideas will be helpful. On the other hand, "IWWMW attract new people to the theater?" and "IWWMW increase season subscribers?" might be combined into a statement such as "H2 attract and retain more theater-goers?"

If you have several hits around a common theme or hot spot, you might find it helpful to use the paraphrase tool (discussed above) to find the best way to state the problem. In this case, you are asking, "Given the common thread or theme in this hot spot or cluster, what would be the best and most concise way to state the problem?"

Summary

The problem statement you select during the focusing phase of Framing Problems might be: one selected from your list; a combination of two or more of the previously listed problem statements that fit together particularly well; or a new problem statement created by paraphrasing a hot spot or cluster from your list. In any case, in Understanding the Challenge, you have selected or constructed a problem statement you can use as you continue your work on the task and your CPS efforts. Table 8 presents some of the Key Questions for Framing Problems.

Generating

- What are some questions for which we would like more ideas?
- What are some questions I would like to look at in a new or different way, or from a new viewpoint or perspective?
- For which question(s) would we like new and unusual ideas?
- Why would I pose this question? Why else?
- What do I hope to gain, accomplish, attain, or resolve?
- What's not the problem?
- What do I really want ideas to be able to do?
- What would I like to produce or generate?
- In What Ways Might I ... (IWWMI ...)
- How Might I ... (HMI ...) or How to (H2 ...) do what?

Focusing

- What's the question for which new ideas would be most helpful?
- Do some questions address similar themes or concerns? Might these be merged into one question?
- What's the "common strand" among the "hits" for me?
- What's the real problem?
- What's the essence of my goals, objectives, or desires?
- What do I (we) most want to search for new possibilities?
- On what question should I begin working?
- What questions suggest the most useful directions?
- Can I paraphrase the main issue of this situation? What is really my (our) most important concern?

Table 8: Some Key Questions for Framing Problems

Chapter 4
Generating Ideas

This component has just one stage, which focuses on producing many new, varied, and unusual ideas. The task may not seem very demanding, but appearances can be deceiving. In just one stage—a single "diamond" within the graphic model on page 15—there resides a very stimulating challenge. It can be, at once, both exhilarating and draining, intellectually, emotionally, and even physically. Groups often desperately need a "break," a time to rest and restock their reservoir of energy, after an intensive idea-generating session.

In the Generating Ideas component, then, your challenge is to wrestle with a problem statement or the focused question on which you're working. It'll be challenging for many reasons, including:

- *It won't just be a matter of remembering.* The ideas you want may not be there waiting for you to recall them. If they were so readily available, it might well not have been a problem for you in the first place. More likely, you will need to bring into being some new ideas, some possibilities that weren't there before.

- *You will be seeking many ideas, not just one.* Opening yourself to the flow of ideas and deliberately searching for a large pool of varied and unusual ideas can be strenuous exercise for any mind.

- *You will surely want a number of possibilities that break new ground.* The chances are good that the obvious ideas may already have been considered, and you're seeking something stronger, more effective, more intriguing. Breaking new ground is not always easy.

- *You will also want to consider ideas that build upon or extend existing strategies, actions, or resources.* Being adaptive and alert to good opportunities to extend or enhance present strengths can also be creatively productive, but challenging.

Generating Ideas provides an opportunity for you to produce many new possibilities for dealing with an open-ended, invitational problem statement. CPS is effective and appropriate for important opportunities and challenges for which you are seeking new and useful options. This component now invites and challenges you to do the thinking that's necessary to find or create those options.

Finally, even though you will hold back judgment or evaluation of ideas during this stage so you will be able to be as productive as possible, you also recognize that a time will soon come when choices and decisions will need to be made. New ideas will eventually have to stand the scrutiny of many tests of reality and acceptance. If you could simply adopt your wildest hopes and dreams, life might be easier. But, mortals that we are, most often the solutions to problems must be able to balance the appeal of newness and innovation with the practical realities and constraints in which we operate. Keeping that balance without "snuffing out" one or the other is demanding.

As you work in Generating Ideas, you will seek many promising new ideas, but you will also have to recognize the need to work on them in preparation for converting them from "good" ideas into "useful" ideas that can be implemented successfully.

Many people seem to equate all of CPS with just Generating Ideas. You may have heard someone say, for example, "We'll do some CPS—let's solve this problem by brainstorming for some new ideas." It isn't that simple, however; idea generation is simply one piece of the whole puzzle. Your process planning efforts will guide you in determining when you need this component and when other stages or components should be considered.

The Generating Phase

You will begin this stage by reviewing your problem statement. That statement, in IWWM ..., HM ..., or H2 ... form, will guide and direct your efforts to generate ideas. Your task in Generating Ideas includes working to produce:

- fluency—many ideas;
- flexibility—a variety of ideas;
- originality—unusual ideas; and
- elaboration—rich, detailed, or complete ideas.

The open-ended, idea-spurring nature of your problem statement is quite likely to stimulate a number of possibilities for many people in the group, even as they read and review it. Be ready to begin capturing those ideas on paper right away.

Remember the ground rules for generating options (from chapter 1), and allow those ideas to flow freely. Do not react to them, judge them, debate their merits or demerits, or even discuss them. In the generating phase of Generating Ideas, the goal is just to come up with as many ideas, and as varied and unique ideas, as possible.

How Many Ideas Should You Seek? Once again, don't just settle for the obvious or easy possibilities that come to mind immediately. The group should push itself to get beyond the ideas that must merely be remembered, dragged up from memory—and to reach for the ideas that have to be constructed or made from scratch. A number of writers in the field have likened this challenge to auto travel, suggesting that we not permit ourselves just to glide along on "mental cruise control." In practice, we have participated in many CPS sessions in which 100 or more ideas were generated, and it is common that at least 30–50 ideas will be generated in order to insure that the group has stretched beyond the obvious possibilities.

In many groups, the ideas will flow steadily, even rapidly, when you are Generating Ideas. Sometimes, in fact, it can be difficult to make sure that all the ideas have been written down. There are other times, however, when the pace is slower and the ideas are much harder to produce. In those times, it is necessary to be able to draw on any of a number of different tools for idea generation. Many of these tools can be useful in restoring the flow of ideas (or stimulating fluency). Others can be particularly useful when a group's thinking seems to have become fixed or locked in a certain direction, so more variety (or flexibility) is desirable. When you wish to encourage more unusual (or original) ideas, or to probe for greater detail (or elaboration), you may want to be able to draw on other techniques. We will highlight just a few of these tools in this chapter; many other resources in the bibliography can be used to expand or build your own working "toolbox for the creative mind." The *Toolbox for Creative Problem Solving* (Isaksen, Dorval, & Treffinger 1998) and *Thinking Tool Guides* (Treffinger & Nassab, 2000) are two resources that present a variety of generating and focusing tools.

Use Idea Checklists. Osborn (1953) described a set of words and phrases, which he called "Idea-Spurring Questions," to help anyone expand or extend his or her search for new ideas. Later, Eberle (1996) organized a number of those questions around a handy, easy-to-remember acronym: SCAMPER. Each letter can remind you of a word or phrase, and one or more related questions, from which new or varied ideas might be suggested for any problem on which you might work. The letters in SCAMPER represent these key words and phrases:

S	ubstitute	What might you use or do instead?
C	ombine	What things might be combined or synthesized to form new ideas?
A	dapt	What might be changed or used in a different way?
M	agnify or Minify	What might be made larger or smaller?
P	ut to Other Uses	How might something be used or applied in a new or different way?
E	liminate	What could be deleted, trimmed away? What might you do without?
R	everse or Rearrange	What if you looked at the problem in the opposite way? What if the parts could be restructured in some other way?

These words and questions can be especially useful when your thinking seems to be "stuck in one place" (that is, all your ideas seem to follow one pattern or direction), and you want to move away or look at the challenge in a new or different way. They might be especially useful, then, when you need to break away from habit-bound thinking, challenge assumptions, or approach the problem from a fresh viewpoint or different perspective.

Use Metaphors or Analogies. When you want to generate some unusual or original possibilities, you may need a strategy that will help you really stretch your mind. For such occasions, we often find that using a metaphor or analogy to expand our thinking is very helpful. Many uses of metaphor and analogy in creative thinking have been developed and described in the "synectics" approaches to creative thinking and problem solving (e.g., Gordon, 1961; Gordon and Poze, 1977).

The term *synectics* means "joining or drawing together of opposites." Metaphor and analogy can stimulate new ideas and connections by taking you away from the familiar characteristics, demands, and assumptions you impose on your problem, examining ideas from a very different case or situation, and then finding ways to draw relevant and original connections from that analog to your problem or task. Often, for example, a metaphor or analogy from nature can be used to identify some new ideas for an interpersonal challenge, for product development or invention, or even for a very technical problem. To one person, observing the clinging together of wet leaves while on a hike in the woods might not mean anything special; but, to another person, they might suggest an important and innovative connection: freeze-drying as an entirely new way of producing potato chips that can be packaged with very little breakage.

When you are working on a problem and struggling to come up with some new ideas, ask yourself if your challenge might be similar to something else in nature (or any other realm that is quite different from that of your problem). What is that other situation? What are some of its important characteristics? How is the problem or challenge handled or resolved in that analog or metaphor? How does it work? What is it that works in that setting? Then, bring those ideas back to your problem. How might you create the same (or parallel) actions or responses in your challenge that work so well in the analogy? What are the common elements in both the metaphor and your challenge? This will often reveal some new and promising ideas that you had not considered.

Use Forced Relationships. The idea of forced relationships involves stimulating original ideas by combining things no one would ordinarily think about as fitting together. One example of this is the force-fitting tool. It involves the ability to see a new possibility in something that, at first glance, appears to have nothing at all to do with your problem—"looking at one thing and seeing something else." If you were asked, "How might you use an alarm clock to improve a lamp?," your first reaction might be to say, "They don't have anything to do with each other. They're entirely different." But, when you begin to play with that combination, some interesting possibilities might arise. How about an alarm clock that automatically turns on the light for you when it's time to wake up? Perhaps it could also be set to turn out the light at a certain time (in case you fall asleep while you're reading this book). You might even be able to use it to turn the light on and off while you're away.

You can apply force fitting or related tools in many ways. Select objects randomly, so you don't impose any preset assumptions on the search for connections. When you need some new ideas, try some of these methods for finding unusual connections:

- Look through a mail order catalog. Select some products at random (leaf through the pages and note the first five things that catch your eye). Now, try to think about what ideas might be suggested for your problem by each of those items, one at a time, or in combinations.

- Take a walk in a shopping mall. Take a pencil or pen and some paper or a small notebook, and jot down five objects at random that you spot in the mall (anywhere, as you walk along). Once again, try to connect each of the objects you select to your problem. Look for some new possibilities.

- Do the same thing at an amusement park, a zoo, or a grocery store.

- Use the classified ads in a newspaper to select some objects at random to search for new connections to your problem.

Use Strategies to Blend Active and Reflective Tools. Sometimes, people have a rather stereotyped image of "brainstorming sessions." They see a group of people, furiously shouting out one idea after another, writing ideas as fast as they possibly can. Sometimes, they see people all talking at once, waving their arms, shouting ideas from every direction. Indeed, sometimes the pace is fast and very energetic (although, with good leadership, we hope it's never as chaotic as the stereotype seems). However, it's important to keep in mind that creativity is not just a frantic pouring forth of ideas all at once. Many people need ample time to reflect about a problem statement before ideas begin to form in their mind. Nearly everyone goes through periods of very intense productivity and other spells of reorganizing and recapturing one's energy and ideas. You will probably find it helpful, then, to allow time for both active idea-generation and for reflection and individual thought. Deliberately providing for some "down time" can also help the search for creative solutions by encouraging time for incubation—the time when you think you're thinking about something else, even though your problem is still being processed while you're unaware of it. (That's what often happens, for example, when you think you've left a problem for the day, but discover that, suddenly and unintentionally, a new idea pops up—in church, at the theater, on the freeway, or in the middle of the night.)

When Focusing Ideas

After you've generated many ideas, you will also need to sort them out and decide which ones you want to carry forward toward forming a solution and designing the actions to take. After generating for many, varied, and unusual ideas, the next phase of the Generating Ideas component and stage calls for focusing.

Focusing your ideas involves identifying the hits in an extensive list of options. Designating some ideas as hits is a way to identify ideas that are promising, warranting further consideration or development. It is a "light" or tentative form of focusing, not a final and unconditional selection of solutions to be implemented.

Ask yourself, "Which of the ideas that have been generated are most intriguing to me? Which ones are the most promising possibilities? Which ones might be best to refine and develop in ways that will help us (me) move forward to a solution and a plan of action?"

Especially in Generating Ideas (but in some ways, in every CPS stage), it is also important when focusing to consider your own style and its implications. Be aware of your own preference or creativity style (e.g., Kirton, 1976).

Are you more adaptive, seeking options to "work within the system," or do things better? In this case, you may tend to identify hits that seem to be safe and comfortable. These may have some advantages. They may be easier to implement than other possibilities, or easier to "sell" to other people. They may build effectively on what already exists in your setting. There is an important caution, though. The ideas you select may not be very new or different from what you've always done in the past, and they might preserve some limitations that hold back progress or growth. They might not respond to the demands of changing times or situations. If, for example, you are the president of a company that makes buggy whips, and you want ideas for improving your revenues, ideas for making even better buggy whips may not be helpful. They might be easy to implement, consistent with your history and traditions, and better than anyone else has ever designed. But, if no one really needs or wants buggy whips in today's world, they won't be ideas that will be likely to lead to much more business or revenue.

On the other hand, if your style is more innovative, you're likely to be drawn more naturally to the newest, most radical ideas—those that are at the cutting edge and might revolutionize the entire field. In this case, you may choose a very different set of promising possibilities. They might be highly original, boundary-breaking innovations. They might help you leap ahead of everyone else in your area. However, there are also some very important pitfalls and cautions here, of which you need to be aware. Your ideas might be very difficult to "sell" to others, both inside your group or organization and outside in the world at large. Many others may be uneasy or uncomfortable with high levels of risk and rapid change. Your ideas might be very difficult and even expensive to implement—and, of course, when you get right down to it, they just might not work. The challenge for you, when you are focusing your ideas, is to remember to keep your feet (well, at least one foot) on the ground, and to avoid getting carried away with wishes and dreams that you will not be able to translate into any kind of practical action at all.

So, ask yourself, "Am I looking for ideas to help me improve or do better what is already happening or existing? If so, which ideas will also help us make progress and move forward?" On the other hand, ask, "Am I looking for the ideas that are really new and different? If so, which ideas can also be made workable?"

Armed with a rich array of new and promising ideas, you will be prepared to consider your next steps.

Summary

Some Key Questions for Generating Ideas are presented in Table 9. Use these to help you keep in mind the important tools, tasks, and strategic considerations for this component.

Generating

- What options and alternatives might there be?
- Can I think of more ways to do it?
- Different ways? New or unusual ways?
- What would I do if there were no obstacles?
- What's my greatest fantasy about how to do this?
- How might this problem be solved?
- What can be used or done in a new way?
- What analogies might help? How do they work?
- How many more possibilities can I create or generate?
- What if the opposite were true?
- What would I wish for in my wildest hopes and dreams?
- Can I visualize or imagine solutions?
- What new connections can I make?
- How might I use some ideas or objects from a totally different context or purpose?

Focusing

- What alternatives are most appealing? Which ones are most attractive?
- What options suggest new and promising ways to solve this problem?
- What ideas do I really like best?
- What ideas surprised me or caught my attention?
- What ideas offered the most unusual, different, or fresh perspective?
- Do some of these ideas go together? Can they be combined, synthesized, or sequenced?
- What ideas deserve closer examination or consideration?
- What ideas offer the best chance to do something?
- Which ideas add value to what already exists? Help make it possible to do things better?
- Which ideas take things in an entirely new direction?

Table 9: Some Key Questions for Generating Ideas

Chapter 5
Preparing for Action

Preparing for Action is primarily concerned with transforming ideas into action. It consists of two specific stages: Developing Solutions and Building Acceptance. Working in this component is important whenever you have promising options or possibilities to refine, analyze, select, or prepare for successful implementation. New ideas are not of much value unless you can insure that they lead to action. If you have ever watched an exciting and unusual new possibility die a cruel death because its creator couldn't (or didn't) convince anyone to put it to use, you are already aware of the importance of this component of CPS.

Developing Solutions

Developing Solutions involves working on promising options to refine or improve them, with the goal of transforming them into possible solutions. A solution is an option or alternative that resolves a problem, answers a question, or meets a challenge. Preparation for Developing Solutions involves clarifying the work that needs to be done with your promising possibilities, and deciding on tools that will be most useful for that work.

Some of the promising options might be very easy to use; perhaps you had not tried them yet simply because you had not thought of them. Now that they have surfaced, they might help you move forward quite readily. There may be other fascinating or appealing possibilities, options that are very unique and in which you can see many strong consequences and results, even though you may not yet have any sense of how (or even whether) they could really be carried out. Developing Solutions will provide the opportunity for you to look at all those promising possibilities more closely or systematically. You might discover that some of the ideas are more promising than others, or you might establish priorities among some of them or a sequence in which to work on them. You might find that many of the ideas (including some of the ones you thought could be used immediately) can be refined or strengthened to overcome limitations or concerns that weren't immediately obvious. You might discover ways to make the most interesting ideas even better. Finally, you might see ways in which some of the ideas might very productively be merged or combined.

Judging options (good or bad? useful or not? practical or unrealistic?) is often the first thing people think about when they look at a brainstormed list: "Okay, now we have all these ideas. Which one is really the best one?" This is not the best way to proceed, for two reasons. First, it forces you unnecessarily and often unproductively, into an either/or mindset. Ideas are not just good or bad; all the ideas might have strengths and weaknesses. Second, your goal is not just to find a single winning idea, but rather to identify any and all possibilities that will help you move forward toward a solution. Your best course of action may draw upon many of the ideas you generated, not just one or two.

The most important point to keep in mind, then, is that Developing Solutions is not merely judging ideas or trying to find one super idea that causes all the others to drop by the wayside. Developing Solutions provides your opportunity to build or mold the most promising options into possible solutions, thus creating a foundation for action that gives you the best possible chance of success.

Begin by examining carefully what really needs to be done. (This is setting your strategy.) Most often, you will consider your first steps along three general pathways:

- *Organizing the possibilities.* Are there so many promising possibilities that you feel overwhelmed? In this case, your challenge will be to sort, compress, or cluster (group) the promising options to make them manageable.

- *Analyzing, refining, or developing possibilities.* If you have a tentative solution before you, your goal in Developing Solutions may be to refine and strengthen it, or to make it the best or strongest solution you can. In this case, your challenge is to apply tools that help you examine thoroughly the strengths and limitations of the possibilities.

- *Choosing among options.* If you have many options that need to be evaluated carefully and in detail, your efforts in Developing Solutions may involve generating, selecting, and applying specific criteria in a well-planned or systematic way to evaluate or prioritize options.

There may also be situations in which you will decide that your Developing Solutions efforts will require you to draw on several of these pathways, not just one. For example, you might need to narrow or compress a number of possibilities and then analyze and refine the cluster that emerges. Or, you may work on refining and developing each of several possibilities, and then prioritize them. Developing Solutions does not necessarily involve a strategy that applies only a single tool.

Generating in Developing Solutions

You may find it helpful to ask yourself, "What makes these possibilities hits? Why are they intriguing to me?" This leads you to think about the criteria that might be both relevant and important in sorting, ranking, developing, or choosing solutions.

Of course, many criteria might be taken into account. In general, we have found it very helpful to remember the simple acronym, CARTS. It represents the following five sets of criteria with some illustrative questions for each set:

Cost. Will the options be cost-effective to implement? Will they require expensive resources? Will it be necessary to obtain many costly resources? Will it exceed our budget or funds available?

Acceptance. Will this possibility be acceptable to others? Will it be acceptable to those who need to support it? Will it be acceptable to the public? Will it be acceptable to me in the long run?

Resources. Will the materials needed be readily available? Will any special support materials or equipment be needed and available to carry out the option?

Time. Will the option fit into our schedule? Will it fit our time requirements? Will it make excessive demands on anyone's time? Will the critical resources and people be available when needed?

Space. Will we have the space or room we need to act on this possibility? Will any special facilities be required and available? Will there be room to do what's needed?

When Developing Solutions, these criteria can help you think clearly and constructively about the factors that may influence the eventual success or failure of your efforts. In that sense, the more criteria you consider, the better, although you must also make certain that the criteria you generate are relevant to your task and goals and that you will still be able to manage your efforts without getting bogged down or confused.

Criteria can be useful or helpful in many ways, depending on what you are seeking to accomplish. For example, consider four different ways you might seek to develop intriguing ideas into solutions: sorting or compressing them (to reduce a large pool of ideas into a more workable set), ranking or prioritizing several ideas, developing and refining promising ideas, or evaluating many ideas in detail. In each case, criteria can be helpful, as illustrated.

If you're working on ...	Criteria can help you to ...
Sorting or compressing ideas	Form hits into hot spots and recognize promising clusters.
Ranking or prioritizing	Weigh one option against another.
Refining and developing	Determine the strengths and limitations accurately.
Evaluating many options	Assess all the options fairly and consistently.

Focusing: Selecting and Applying Helpful Tools

Several different focusing tools can be very helpful when you are Developing Solutions. Their selection and appropriate application depends on the results of your process planning. Depending on what you're seeking to accomplish, there are three major pathways, and there may be times when you will follow more than one of them. In general, the three pathways involve developing options, narrowing options, or evaluating options. Each involves different strategies.

- *Working with a few significant options.* In some circumstances, you may have one or two really powerful options that appeal very strongly—possibilities that really stand "head and shoulders" above any others. (This might be one or two hot spots or clusters, too; it doesn't have to be limited to separate or isolated ideas or options.) When there have been a few highly significant or powerful possibilities, and you find that you can and will put all of those ideas to use, you might think that Developing Solutions will not be important or necessary. But, when you remember that Developing Solutions involves refining and strengthening options, not just judging them, its importance is clear. In this case, your goal is to make certain the promising options or clusters are really as complete, strong, and polished as you can make them.

In this situation, we recommend using a Developing Solutions tool that helps you to strengthen or improve the idea or cluster. You might choose, for example, the ALoU tool (Isaksen, Dorval, & Treffinger, 1998).

ALoU Tool

A dvantages
L imitations (o=overcome)
U nique Qualities

For the option or cluster you wish to develop, begin by listing the good features, strengths, or advantages of the idea. These are the advantages (A in ALoU). It is important to begin with these so you can establish a constructive or affirmative approach and outlook.

You will also explore the option's unique qualities or potentials (U in ALoU). These are long-term (or "upstream") benefits—the good things that might come about or be made possible as a result or consequence of the option you're reviewing now, or the aspects of the options that are unique and really make it appealing.

In addition, you will identify possible limitations or concerns (the L in ALoU). These are the potential weakness, liabilities, or limitations that will need to be considered before using the option. To prevent the limitations or concerns from becoming idea killers, we recommend you state them in "How to …" or "How might we …" form. Expressing the concerns as mini-problem statements reminds you that you can seek ways to overcome them. After you have identified these limitations, select those of particular concern and devote some time and effort to seeking ways to prevent or overcome them. The "o" reminds you to look for ways to overcome those limitations.

When using the ALoU tool, criteria can be used to help you recognize and define the advantages, limitations, and unique qualities.

- *Ranking or prioritizing.* The second common case that results from Generating Ideas is having identified a few hits or hot spots, but also having recognized that you may not be able to use or carry out all of them. For many reasons (limitations of time, personnel, other resources, or efficiency, for example), it might not be feasible to implement all of the promising possibilities. It might also be possible that the promising ideas overlap in their purposes or results, so that trying to implement more than one would probably be unnecessary or redundant. Thus, your concern in this case will be to decide which of the promising possibilities might be best to use first, or which one might have the greatest likelihood of success.

For this situation, we recommend the use of the Paired Comparison Analysis (PCA) tool (Treffinger, Isaksen, & Firestien, 1982; Isaksen & Treffinger, 1985; Isaksen, Dorval, & Treffinger, 1998; Treffinger & Nassab, 2000). The PCA tool guides you in comparing each one of your promising possibilities with each other, one pair at a time, until all possible pairs have been compared. It is easiest to use when you are working with a relatively small number of possibilities (as a rule of thumb, fewer than 10); with a larger number, the total number of pairs to be compared with each other increases greatly and can become laborious and confusing.

To use the PCA tool, make a grid in which you list the ideas to be compared—your most promising possibilities from Generating Ideas—across the columns and down the rows. (The same ideas appear in both the columns and the rows.) See Figure 5 for an example.

Note the diagonal row of Xs. Each comparison marked by an X is not used, since it would be meaningless to compare an idea with itself. Also, there is no need to make any of the comparisons under the Xs, since they simply repeat a comparison that was made above the Xs. (Comparing B with A is the same, for example, as comparing A with B.) Each pair of letters in each cell above the Xs (A-B, A-C, B-C, B-D, C-D, C-E, D-E, etc.) represents a specific comparison of one pair of your promising possibilities. For five options, you will make 10 specific comparisons.

For each pair you compare, think about the criteria you have determined are important, and choose one of the two. Circle your choice. For example, as you consider your criteria and compare Option A and Option B, which one do you consider stronger or more likely to be useful and successful? If it's A, circle A; if B, circle B.

	Option A	Option B	Option C	Option D	Option E
Option A	X	A-B	A-C	A-D	A-E
Option B		X	B-C	B-D	B-E
Option C			X	C-D	C-E
Option D				X	D-E
Option E					X

Figure 6: PCA (Paired Comparison Analysis) Tool

When you have completed all 10 paired comparisons, you will be able to count the choices you have made, and thus establish the ranking or priorities among your five choices, when compared to each other. (More complex variations of this tool can be used; for example, the choices for each pair can be weighted as to the magnitude or strength of preference.)

- *Evaluating and selecting from many options.* The third situation occurs when, as a result of a very exciting and productive Generating Ideas experience, you have so many intriguing and promising possibilities that you don't know what to do with them all. This case challenges you to examine the options very carefully, considering the details that will help you see where the greatest potentials might be.

Under these circumstances, you might find it most helpful to use an Evaluation Matrix to examine the options. To use this tool, construct a matrix in which you enter the criteria you have developed in the columns (one criterion per column), and then enter one of your promising possibilities in each row of the matrix. (Remember: columns are vertical, rows are horizontal.) The result might look like Figure 7.

There might be any number of criteria, and any number of options (represented by "... ...") in the illustration).

Next, examine each of the options using the criteria. We recommend looking at one criterion at a time. Examine each of the options using that criterion, and then proceed to the next criterion. This will help you insure that you apply each criterion fairly and consistently to all the options. There are several ways to apply the criteria. You might simply enter for each row a word or phrase (e.g., "good," "fair," or "poor") or a symbol to represent those words. You might use a numerical evaluation scale (e.g., from 1 [poor] to 5 [excellent]). You might use more complex systems, such as one in which different weights are given to each criterion, depending on your judgment of its overall importance.

When you have applied all the criteria to all the options, you can review the results to examine the options and determine your next steps. Once again, remember that this procedure does not have to result in the selection of only one option. You might identify several options to be used immediately, others that might be modified or held for later use, or some that might be combined for greater impact or value.

	Criterion 1 Cost	Criterion 2 Acceptance	Criterion 3 Time	Criterion 4 (... ...) Space
Option 1				
Option 2				
Option 3				
... ...				
Option N				

Figure 7: Sample Evaluation Matrix

Summary

Table 10 presents some key questions to consider for Developing Solutions. Keep in mind, once again, that the we's and the me's will vary, depending on whether the client, or owner of the task, is an individual or a group.

Generating

- What needs to be done to refine, develop, or choose possible solutions?
- What standards or "yardsticks" might be applied to these options?
- What factors might be most useful and important to consider in comparing, developing, modifying, or improving these options?
- How might interesting options be made stronger or better?
- How might fantasy ideas be made more realistic?
- What makes some possibilities less interesting or attractive?
- Why are we (am I) pushed toward some option and away from others?
- What new directions or concerns might be suggested?

- What are the appealing features of all the ideas? How might these be combined or interchanged among ideas?

Focusing Using Appropriate Tools

- What tool(s) will be most helpful to use?
- What criteria might be useful and important to consider?
- What are the Advantages, Limitations, and Unique Qualities of these options? How might you overcome the limitations?
- Which possibilities should have the highest ranking or priority?
- How do the options measure up or compare—with each other?
- With specific criteria or standards of evaluation?
- Do the options really satisfy important needs and concerns?
- What options (or combinations) are most promising?
- Which ones will really get the job done for me (us)?

Table 10: Some Key Questions for Developing Solutions

Building Acceptance

Building Acceptance challenges you to look at promising solutions through the eyes of others and to examine your solutions in ways that will lead to action. In this stage, you will direct your efforts toward investigating ways to increase or enhance assistance and support for the solutions, and minimizing or counteracting objections or resistance. Finally, you will be guided in making decisions and planning specific steps, both short- and long-term, to gain support for, carry out, and evaluate actions.

You have probably witnessed or experienced many situations in which an idea that seemed to be a very good, promising solution did not have great success or impact. Ideas often "die on the vine" from lack of follow-through, commitment, or from not receiving the support they need for continuity and long-term results. These situations remind us very clearly that there can be a great difference between good ideas and useful solutions. Building Acceptance is an important stage in which you will make serious efforts to insure that your good ideas become useful solutions.

Generating When Building Acceptance

When Building Acceptance, generating involves looking carefully at promising solutions in an effort to assess what will be necessary for them to be carried into action successfully. To accomplish this, it can be very helpful to explore possible assisters and resisters for implementation.

Identify Possible Assisters. What will have to happen to make the solution work the way you hope or wish it could? This involves searching for Assisters. Assisters might be the helpful people upon whom you will depend for success. Who else besides yourself will support the promising solution(s) you have created? Who else needs to support them? Are there some "key players" whose support must be won?

Assisters are not only people, they are also anything that will help improve your chances of successful action. You might use the 5 Ws (discussed in chapter 3), but in a unique way in relation to Building Acceptance. For example:

Who?	Helpful people.
What?	The essential resources or things you will need for successful action.
When?	The best times to carry out your ideas.
Where?	The best places to implement the plans.
Why?	The best, most important, or most persuasive justifications for your ideas.

Identify Possible Resisters. Don't fall into the old trap of convincing yourself that "nothing could possibly go wrong." Very few ideas are ever fool-proof, and the newer and more original they are, the greater the chances not only that something can go wrong—but that it will! The wise problem solver (that's you) accepts this dose of reality, and takes precautions accordingly. Resisters are people, places, things, times, or actions that might go wrong or create difficulties. Once again, consider the 5 Ws:

Who?	Critics or opponents. Who might have something to lose if the idea works or something to gain if it fails? Who might be threatened or uncomfortable in dealing with the idea?
What?	What important things or resources might be missing, unavailable when you need them, lost, or overlooked?
When?	The worst possible times to carry out your ideas.
Where?	The worst places to implement the plans.
Why?	The least persuasive justifications for your ideas. Why might people turn away from the ideas?

You might deal with possible resisters in two ways. First, you can try to anticipate them, so that, if it is at all possible, you can avoid or prevent them from occurring. Second, if you can't prevent them, you can at least consider possible ways to deal with them or overcome them if they do occur.

Building Acceptance also involves another kind of generating: working on generating a number of possible specific Action Steps to take in carrying out your solution. These steps will take into account your thoughts about Assisters and Resisters. Before you define the Action Steps specifically, you will probably find it helpful to engage in some initial focusing efforts.

Focusing When Building Acceptance

After you have listed many possible Assisters and Resisters, focusing involves asking, "Which ones are the most likely and important to deal with?" Select several key Assisters, and note how you will make better use of them. Then, select some of the most significant possible Resisters. Which ones are most likely to arise? Which ones would have the worst impact on your success? Consider several ideas for preventing them or responding to them. You will occasionally identify something or someone as potentially both an Assister and a Resister. In this case, consider ways to maximize the assistance, and thereby minimize the resistance.

After you have generated possible Action Steps, your focus may shift to deciding which of those steps you will actually decide to take, and how, when, and where you will take them. How will you gain support for your solutions? What will you need to do to carry out these solutions? How will you evaluate your actions?

In Building Acceptance, then, you will often find that you are generating and focusing in several ways and more than once, depending on the situation's complexity and demands. You will generate when you identify possible Assisters and Resisters, and focus when you determine which ones are probable and significant. You may generate to consider possible action steps, and focus by deciding what steps are the best to take.

A strong focusing step when Building Acceptance is developing a specific, detailed Plan of Action. What are the steps you are committed to taking? What resources will be required to take them? When and where will they take place? Who will be involved? Why are they important? How will you carry them out? You might begin with an overall description of your intended actions, such as a statement that begins, "What I see myself doing to solve this problem is …." Don't stop at this general level. We recommend that you include three specific levels of action in your plan:

The 24-Hour Steps. The longer you wait before you act, the less likely it becomes that you will take any action. Therefore, identify at least one or two concrete steps you can take—right away, within the next 24 hours, without fail (no excuses!). Make the commitment to begin— "By this time tomorrow, I will have …."

Short-Term Steps. Next, identify several short-term steps that will move your plan forward. How soon is short term? It depends on you, on the steps, on the overall time plan, on the problem itself. Decide what you will consider "short term," express it clearly, and define the steps to take in that time frame. List the time frame and the action (for example, "By this time next week, I will have ….").

Long-Term Steps. Finally, define "long term," depending on your overall schedule and the demands of the situation, and list the specific actions you will take.

Certainly, depending on what happens as you implement any of the steps in your Plan of Action, it can become necessary to rethink the plan, revise it, and delete some steps or add others. You control the Plan of Action, and you can modify it at any time. It is important to have a plan to begin with, so you will have a good record of what you have done, what has (or hasn't) been successful, and what needs to be done next. You must also consider how you will evaluate your plans and the actions you take

Often it is helpful to identify a friend or colleague with whom you can share your Plan of Action. This person can serve in the role of a "friendly nag," reminding you of the action commitments you have set for yourself.

Summary

A Plan of Action should help you define clearly what you're going to do (and when, where, and how) in order to implement your most promising solution or response(s) for your task. Table 11 presents some key questions for Building Acceptance.

Generating

- How might promising solutions be implemented?
- What might be sources of assistance or resistance?
- What might make action easier to take? More difficult?
- What are some possible obstacles, objections, or concerns?
- What might go right? So what?
- What might go wrong? So what?
- How might implementation problems be avoided?
- What might we do if problems arise anyway?
- What help might be needed? From whom? How obtained?
- What might be the best thing that could happen? The worst?
- What might stall, delay, or interfere with your plans?
- Who or what could make your action a "breeze"?

Focusing

- What's most likely to help you implement your Plan of Action?
- Who or what are the key Assisters?
- What's most likely to hinder successful implementation of your Plan of Action?
- Who or what are the key Resisters?
- What specific actions are necessary within 24 hours?
- What's short term, and what should be done then?
- What's long term, and what should be done then?
- How do we start? Where? By when? What deadlines?
- How might you prevent problems?
- What are the most likely contingent steps if problems arise?
- How will you monitor and document your progress?
- How will you evaluate your actions?

Table 11: Some Key Questions for Building Acceptance

Chapter 6

Applying CPS

The major purposes of this chapter are to define some of the important factors that contribute to success in applying CPS and to help you identify several ways to increase your confidence and proficiency in using CPS.

After you've completed studying this book, we're confident that you will have a good, fundamental understanding of what CPS is, and that you will be sufficiently confident and eager to try out CPS methods and tools to deal with many problems and challenges in your own personal or professional setting. You probably will not feel like an expert in CPS, but that should not prevent you from getting started on your own. This chapter will provide a number of suggestions to help you to get started.

Debriefing

People who use CPS regularly find that they learn a number of new things every time they work on a problem. There are always new insights. Sometimes, for example, you might try some things you have never tried before—just a little experiment that occurs to you while you're working. Whether it was successful or not, there is still something to learn from the experience.

After every CPS application, then, we sit down to review the session, engaging in what we describe as debriefing. This is a deliberate process in which we address such questions as:

- What went well? What were the best parts of what took place?
- Why did I do certain things during the session? What were my reactions and those of others if in a group session?
- What could have been improved or handled more effectively?
- How could the session have been made better or more productive?
- Were there any interesting things in this session that we've never discovered before? What were they? How did they work? How might they best be incorporated into future efforts?

What Contributes To Success in Applying CPS?

Through many years of research, development, and experience with CPS groups, we have identified a number of factors contributing to success. These include: Warm-Up; Remembering and Following the Basic Ground Rules; Important Logistics; Time; Appropriate Teamwork and Group Dynamics; Role Definition and Clarity; and Idea Support.

Warm-Up

Dr. E. Paul Torrance of the University of Georgia has long stressed the importance of taking time for "warm up" or preparation for creative thinking. One way to get yourself ready to think creatively is to give yourself a challenge for open-ended or divergent thinking before starting work on a real problem. Look out a window or at an interesting picture, or listen to some music, for example. Ask, "What do I see? What do I hear? What else might there be?" Stretch yourself deliberately to think of several possibilities.

Remembering and Following the Basic Ground Rules

The success of many CPS efforts has been influenced very strongly by the willingness and ability of all group members to keep in mind and follow the basic ground rules (see chapter 1). The attitudes of Deferred and Affirmative Judgment are important in creating and maintaining a productive climate for problem solving. We recommend that you always begin any CPS session with a brief review and reminder about these ground rules.

Important Logistics

When you are planning to use CPS, by yourself or with a group, there are some practical concerns to keep in mind. Do you have everything you need to get started? Do you have the tools you will need for a productive meeting, including plenty of flip chart paper and markers?

Treffinger and Firestien (1989) offered a number of practical suggestions for conducting an effective CPS application, considering the props and materials needed to insure that things run smoothly, and creating an environment that supports and stimulates productive thinking. These suggestions are summarized below.

- Use large sheets of flip chart paper or newsprint (24" by 36" works well) for a convenient and permanent record of your ideas. Don't rely on overheads or chalkboards, which can easily be erased and may be difficult to review as your work progresses.

- If you don't have an easel, use masking tape to attach the paper to a wall or chalkboard. Use several columns of paper, so you can easily move across the wall while writing. Also, use layers of paper several sheets thick; pauses to put up more paper will be brief, and the danger of ink bleeding through to the wall is decreased.

- Large crayons can often be just as useful as ink markers. They're less expensive, and they don't bleed through the paper.

- When working in a group, arrange all the chairs into a horseshoe or U-shape, so everyone can easily see the easel or the wall with the paper on it—and each other.

- Number and label each sheet as you begin writing on it (e.g., Framing Problems #1, or "PF-1"). After the meeting, it will be easier to review the sequence of ideas and events.

- Number every idea as you go along to make it easier to identify hot spots when focusing.

- Throughout any CPS application, keep the previous sheets in sight. You may want to look back from time to time to review prior ideas or thoughts.

- Record all ideas as accurately as possible; don't try to edit or correct anyone's ideas as you record them. (Teachers: don't slip into grammar lessons in the midst of a CPS application!)

- Use a back up person as a recorder, or provide large Post-it® notes for participants, so idea production doesn't get bogged down waiting for ideas to be recorded. (Provide paper and pencils for all group members, too.)

- Don't depend on a tape recorded version of the meeting. They can be very difficult to understand and transcribe, especially when the ideas from several members of a group are flowing rapidly.

Time

How much time do you need for applying any components or stages of CPS? This seems like an innocent, simple question, but it is really much more complex than it appears. The time you will need depends on several factors, including:

- *The nature and magnitude of the task or challenge.* There are two-minute problems, two-hour problems, and so on—probably up to and including "two-lifetime" problems.

- *Your ownership and involvement.* The stronger your involvement in and commitment to the problem, the less concerned you will be about the time needed, no matter how much time is required.

- *Your decisions regarding selection and management of components and stages.* You may need to work with any of the CPS components or stages, and your choices (in advance, and as you proceed) will influence the amount of time you will need.

- The number of meetings or total amount of time available. Even if you were to apply all three CPS components in order to deal effectively with a certain problem, it would not be necessary (and may well not be advisable) to attempt to do everything in one session. You might consider spreading your efforts over several consecutive working meetings and providing additional time for monitoring your progress and the need for various components or stages. There may also be times when you must work under extreme time pressures or emergency constraints, in which case you must react and respond very quickly. Under such circumstances, any CPS tools you can remember and apply may help you function as effectively as possible.

Appropriate Teamwork and Group Dynamics

The effectiveness and impact of CPS can be enhanced considerably when the members of a group are aware of the impact of style differences within the group, and the need for teamwork, supportive interpersonal behavior, and good communication skills.

Role Definition and Clarity

There are four important roles in a CPS session: the client, the resource group members, the facilitator, and the process buddy. Your CPS efforts will be more successful when participants understand these roles and the responsibilities that accompany them. Everyone—in all four basic roles—shares responsibility for a successful application CPS.

- *Client.* The client is the person (or, sometimes, the group) who owns the problem. The client is responsible for taking action on the problem and has the ability and intent of doing so. It is the client's problem on which a CPS group will be working. Depending on the component or stage in which you are working, the client's role can include defining the opportunity or challenge, providing data, participating actively in the generating phase of any CPS stage, and guiding the group in focusing. Since the client is the one responsible for action, he or she (or they) must be respected and supported in the focusing phases.

- *Resource Group Members.* The resource group members are the people who have agreed to participate in using CPS (in addition to the client and the facilitator). Their primary role is to participate actively in the generating phase of any CPS stage. They serve as the "think tank," helping the client generate ideas that provide new perspectives, variety, and uniqueness—going beyond the ideas the client might already have had.

- *Facilitator.* The facilitator is the trained person who manages the operation and progress of the CPS work. It is best for the facilitator to be detached from the content of the meeting, so she or he can focus entirely on the group's needs and program management.

- *Process Buddy.* The process buddy might be any member of the group who, at any time, assists and supports the group in managing environmental conditions or session logistics. The process buddy can also support the facilitator by being alert to the dynamics of the group, or of particular group members, at any time during the session.

Idea Support

The success of any CPS application is also enhanced by the group's willingness and ability to provide extended effort and to apply a variety of different strategies, tools, and techniques as they may be needed. The group will also function more effectively when all group members feel comfortable building on each other's ideas, and when they can do so in good humor—maintaining an environment that is playful in attitude, but serious in purpose.

Learning and Applying CPS in Many Settings

We have found that CPS can be used successfully for a wide range of problems or challenges, including: individuals or groups; personal or professional problems; and people problems, product problems, or planning problems. CPS has been used across many ages, from children five or six years of age in the primary grades (e.g., Keller-Mathers & Puccio, 2000; Puccio, Keller-Mathers, & Treffinger, 2000) to adults (actively involved in, or retired from) the corporate, business, or professional worlds (e.g., Isaksen, Dorval, & Treffinger, 1994, 1998). With any age group or in any setting, the challenge of learning and applying CPS effectively involves several dimensions. Treffinger and Feldhusen (1998) offered a model, which is presented in Figure 8, for teaching and learning productive thinking that also applies specifically to CPS.

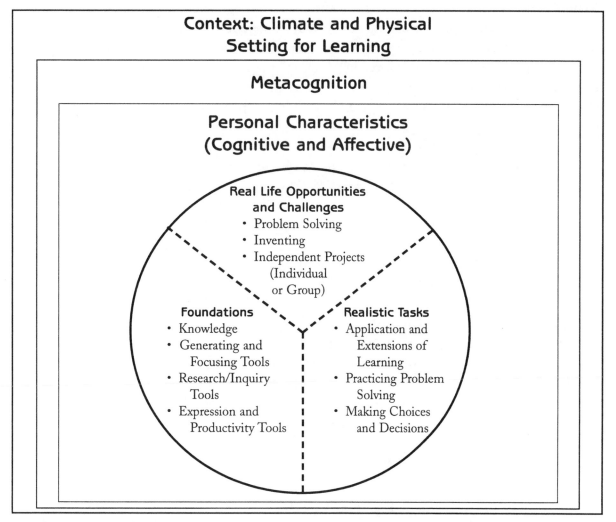

Figure 8: Model for Teaching and Learning Productive Thinking (Treffinger & Feldhusen, 1998, p. 27)

Creative Problem Solving: An Introduction

Three general dimensions must always be considered: the context or environment for teaching and learning, metacognitive skills (monitoring, managing, and modifying your thinking while you are in process), and personal characteristics (including cognitive abilities, specific talents and interests, personal characteristics, and style preferences, for example). Then, in the center of the model, Treffinger and Feldhusen described three important dimensions of teaching and learning: the foundations, realistic tasks, and real-life opportunities and challenges. Although instruction or training in CPS might treat these as sequential, it is not necessarily always the case that they will (or should) follow a single, sequential pattern. There may be many instances, for example, when work on a real-life problem clarifies the need for new "foundations," tools, or skills. For simplicity of presentation, however, we will summarize each of the three dimensions, beginning with the foundations.

Foundations. As a foundation for CPS, it is helpful for people to learn and use a number of basic tools for generating or focusing options and for process management. These tools can be learned in many ways. Although there has been debate in the field of thinking skills regarding "direct" versus "content-embedded" teaching of tool skills, we believe that both can be valuable. Many of the tools can be learned quickly and easily through the use of contrived exercises or activities that draw upon the common, everyday experiences familiar to most people. These direct instructional efforts may not represent the person's actual context for applying and using the tools—the domain or content area in which the person works—but they often help people recognize that the tools can be applied in a variety of different contexts. Direct instruction can always be followed, or even accompanied by, deliberate efforts to practice and apply the tools in context-relevant applications.

Many published programs and materials can be used to support direct instruction in the foundation tools. Feldhusen and Treffinger (1985) reviewed several tools and a number of programs for school use. Treffinger, Feldhusen, Isaksen, Cross, Remle, and Sortore (1993) provided an extensive set of criteria for reviewing and evaluating published resources, with reviews of more than 50 published materials. Isaksen, Dorval, and Treffinger (1998), and Treffinger and Nassab (2000) developed instructional materials and trainers' resources for teaching a variety of basic tools that are linked directly to the CPS approach.

Realistic Tasks. The foundational tools certainly can become more valuable and powerful when they are incorporated into the larger CPS framework. In the "realistic" dimension of the model for teaching and learning productive thinking, the primary goals involve learning and practicing the CPS components and stages. Realistic experiences, such as "packaged" practice problems, help to expand and build upon the foundation tools. The importance of this foundation might be expressed through three key words:

- competence—knowing CPS;
- confidence—belief in your ability to use CPS successfully; and
- commitment—seeking opportunities to use CPS.

The realistic dimension sometimes involves the use of contrived practice problems or exercises for any of the CPS components or stages. They may take the form of simulations, case studies, video clips or dramatizations of brief scenarios, or printed exercises. Realistic practice problems are intended to use content that will be of interest to the students, even though it is not of direct personal importance or consequence. The goal is to provide problems that are sufficiently engaging to be motivating for the group, but not so intensely involving that the group's investment in solving the problem makes it difficult for them to learn and practice appropriate CPS tools. No one expects that anyone will actually use or do anything with the solutions that are created, because the problems are imaginary. Thus, we describe them as "realistic" problems, rather than as real problems. For example, Treffinger (2000) provided a collection of 50 sample problems suitable for use with children and teenagers.

Real Life Opportunities and Challenges. No one learns CPS simply as an interesting academic exercise, or just for the opportunity to do "practice problems" that are contrived and provided by a teacher, trainer, or workshop leader. The reason most people learn CPS is to increase their ability to think productively (creatively and critically) in situations that really matter in their life and work.

Unlike the contrived, practice problems sometimes employed in the realistic dimension, real problems are the authentic opportunities, challenges, and concerns people encounter in real life. Real problems are situations that you really care about; you feel strongly about them, and you want to be able to solve them. You intend, without any doubt, to put the solutions to work and carry out your results. Working on real problems, not just realistic exercises, is the eventual goal of any instructional or training program in CPS.

The three central dimensions of this model can guide your planning efforts to help anyone, at any age or in any setting, learn CPS and make it an important and useful part of their life and work.

Summary

We have now completed our overview of Creative Problem Solving. This book can be a useful resource to you in your efforts to understand and use:

- ground rules and specific tools for generating and focusing options;
- structured procedures for determining the relevance and need for CPS methods, and for selecting and managing CPS components and stages; and
- natural, flexible, and dynamic methods for Understanding the Challenge (including Constructing Opportunities, Exploring Data, and Framing Problems); Generating Ideas; and Preparing for Action (including Developing Solutions and Building Acceptance).

The book has also sought to guide you as you consider the important roles within a CPS group, several factors that influence your success in using CPS, and a systematic approach to teaching and learning CPS. CPS provides a set of powerful tools to draw upon and apply in varied ways, but we hope you will not think of it as a rigidly prescribed, fixed set of steps that must be followed mechanically. Finally, working with CPS will give you a systematic approach to problem solving, to use on your own and as you work with others.

Productive thinking and Creative Problem Solving involve more than learning a few quick tricks. As you become involved in this framework, you will discover a life-long journey that is challenging, ever-changing, and always offering new opportunities for growth. We hope you will find the journey rewarding, and we invite you to contact us to share your successes and your questions.

Bibliography

I. References Cited In Text

Eberle, B. (1996). *SCAMPER*. Waco, TX: Prufrock Press.

Feldhusen, J. F., & Treffinger, D. J. (1985). *Creative thinking and problem solving in gifted education* (3rd ed.), Dubuque, IA: Kendall/Hunt.

Firestien, R. L. (1988). From basics to breakthroughs. Buffalo, NY: DOK.

Firestien, R. L., & Treffinger, D. J. (1983). Ownership and converging: Essential ingredients of creative problem solving. *Journal of Creative Behavior, 17*, 32–38.

Gordon, W. J. J. (1961). *Synectics*. New York: Harper & Row.

Gordon, W. J. J., & Poze, T. (1977). *The metaphorical way of learning and knowing*. Cambridge, MA: Porpoise Books.

Isaksen, S. G., & Deschryver, L. (2000). Making a difference with CPS: A summary of the evidence. In S. G. Isaksen (Ed.) *Facilitative Leadership: Making a difference with CPS*. Dubuque, IA: Kendall-Hunt.

Isaksen, S. G., Dorval, K. B., & Treffinger, D. J. (1994). *Creative approaches to problem solving*. Dubuque, IA: Kendall/Hunt.

Isaksen, S. G., Dorval, K. B., & Treffinger, D. J. (1998). *Toolbox for creative problem solving*. Williamsville, NY: Creative Problem Solving Group—Buffalo.

Isaksen, S. G., Murdock, M. C., Firestien, R. L., & Treffinger, D. J. (Eds.). (1993a). *Understanding and recognizing creativity: Emergence of a discipline*. Norwood, NJ: Ablex.

Isaksen, S. G., Murdock, M. C., Firestien, R. L., & Treffinger, D. J. (Eds.). (1993b). *Nurturing and developing creativity: Emergence of a discipline*. Norwood, NJ: Ablex.

Isaksen, S. G., & Treffinger, D. J. (1985). *Creative problem solving: The basic course*. Buffalo, NY: Bearly Limited.

Isaksen, S. G., Treffinger, D. J., & Dorval, K. B. (1997). *The creative problem solving framework: An historical perspective.* Sarasota, FL: Center for Creative Learning.

Keller-Mathers, S., & Puccio, K. (2000). *Big tools for young thinkers.* Waco, TX: Prufrock Press.

Osborn, A. F. (1953). *Applied imagination.* New York: Scribners.

Parnes, S. J. (1967). *Creative behavior guidebook.* New York: Scribners.

Parnes, S. J. (1981). *The magic of your mind.* Buffalo, NY: Creative Education Foundation.

Parnes, S. J. (1987). The creative studies project. In S. G. Isaksen (Ed.), *Frontiers of creativity research: Beyond the basics* (pp. 156–188). Buffalo, NY: Bearly Limited.

Parnes, S. J., Noller, R. B., & Biondi, A. M. (1977). *Guide to creative action.* New York: Scribners.

Puccio, K., Keller-Mathers, S., & Treffinger, D. J. (2000). *Adventures in real problem solving.* Waco, TX: Prufrock Press.

Rose, L. H., & Lin, H. T. (1984). A meta-analysis of long-term creativity training programs. *Journal of Creative Behavior, 18,* 11–22.

Torrance, E. P. (1972). Can we teach children to think creatively? *Journal of Creative Behavior, 6,* 114–143.

Torrance, E. P. (1987). Recent trends in teaching children and adults to think creatively. In S. G. Isaksen (Ed.), *Frontiers of creativity research: Beyond the basics* (pp. 204–215). Buffalo, NY: Bearly Limited.

Treffinger, D. J. (1984). *Creative and critical thinking: Mutually important components of effective problem solving.* Baltimore, MD: State Education Dept., Office on Gifted and Talented.

Treffinger, D. J. (1994). *The real problem solving handbook.* Sarasota, FL: Center for Creative Learning.

Treffinger, D. J. (1997). Toward a more precise, concise, and consistent language for productive thinking instruction. *Creative Learning Today, 7(1),* 1, 8–9.

Treffinger, D. J. (2000). *CPS practice problems* (3rd ed.). Waco, TX: Prufrock Press.

Treffinger, D. J., & Feldhusen, J. F. (1998). *Planning for productive thinking and learning.* Sarasota, FL: Center for Creative Learning.

Treffinger, D. J., Feldhusen, J. F., Isaksen, S. G., Cross, J. A., Jr., Remle, R. C., & Sortore, M. R. (1993). *Productive thinking: Handbook I—Foundations, criteria, and program reviews.* Sarasota, FL: Center for Creative Learning.

Treffinger, D. J., & Firestien, R. L. (1989a). Guidelines for effective facilitation of Creative Problem Solving. *Gifted Child Today, 12*(4), 35–39.

Treffinger, D. J., & Firestien, R. L. (1989b). Guidelines for effective facilitation of Creative Problem Solving. *Gifted Child Today, 12*(5), 44–47.

Treffinger, D. J., & Firestien, R. L. (1989c). Guidelines for effective facilitation of Creative Problem Solving. *Gifted Child Today, 12*(6), 40–44.

Treffinger, D. J., Isaksen, S. G., & Firestien, R. L. (1982). *Handbook of creative learning: Vol. 1.* Honeoye, NY: Center for Creative Learning.

Treffinger, D. J., Isaksen, S. G., & Firestien, R. L. (1983). Theoretical perspectives on creative learning and its facilitation: An overview. *Journal of Creative Behavior, 17,* 9–7.

Treffinger D. J., & Nassab, C. A. (2000). *Thinking tool guides.* Waco, TX: Prufrock Press.

II. Other Related Readings

Basadur, M. (1987). Needed research in creativity for business and industrial applications. In S. G. Isaksen (Ed.), *Frontiers of creativity research: Beyond the basics* (pp. 390–416). Buffalo, NY: Bearly Limited.

Dunn, R., Dunn, K., & Treffinger, D. J. (1992). *Bringing out the giftedness in your child.* New York: Wiley.

Eberle, B., & Stanish, B. (1996a). *Be a problem solver.* Waco, TX: Prufrock Press.

Eberle, B., & Stanish, B. (1996b). *CPS for kids.* Waco, TX: Prufrock Press.

Elwell, P. (1994). *CPS for teens.* Waco, TX: Prufrock Press.

Huber, J. R., Treffinger, D. J., Tracy, D. B., & Rand D. C. (1979). Self-instructional use of programmed creativity training materials with gifted and regular students. *Journal of Educational Psychology, 71,* 303–309.

Isaksen, S. G. (1983). Toward a model for the facilitation of creative problem solving. *Journal of Creative Behavior, 17,* 18–31.

Isaksen, S. G. (1984). Implications of creativity for middle school education. Transessence. *The Journal of Emerging Adolescent Education, 12*, 13–27.

Isaksen, S. G. (Ed.). (1987). *Frontiers of creativity research: Beyond the basics.* Buffalo, NY: Bearly Limited.

Isaksen, S. G. (1988a). Educational implications of creativity research: An updated rationale for creative learning. In K. Grønhaug & G. Kaufmann (Eds.), *Innovation: A cross-disciplinary perspective* (pp. 167–203). Oslo: Norwegian University Press.

Isaksen, S. G. (1988b). Human factors for innovative problem solving. In R. L. Kuhn (Ed.), *Handbook for creative and innovative managers* (pp. 139–146). New York: McGraw-Hill.

Isaksen, S. G., & Parnes, S. J. (1985). Curriculum planning for creative thinking and problem solving. *Journal of Creative Behavior, 19*, 1–29.

Isaksen, S. G., & Treffinger, D. J. (1991). Creative learning and problem solving. In A. Costa (Ed.), *Developing minds: Programs for teaching thinking* (Rev. ed., Vol. 2, pp. 89–93). Alexandria, VA: Association for Supervision and Curriculum Development.

Kirton, M. J. (1976). Adaptors and innovators: A description and measure. *Journal of Applied Psychology, 61*, 622–629.

Mansfield, R. S., Busse, T. V., & Krepelke, E. J. (1978). The effectiveness of creativity training. *Review of Educational Research, 48*, 517–536.

Meadow, A., & Parnes, S. J. (1959). Evaluation of training in creative problem solving. *Journal of Applied Psychology, 43*, 189–194.

Meadow, A., Parnes, S. J., & Reese, H. R. (1959). Influence of brainstorming instructions and problem sequence on a creative problem solving test. *Journal of Applied Psychology, 43*, 413–416.

Noller, R. B., Parnes, S. J., & Biondi, A. M. (1976). *Creative action book.* New York: Scribners.

Parnes, S. J. (1961). The effects of extended effort in creative problem solving. *Journal of Educational Psychology, 52*, 117–122.

Parnes, S. J. (Ed.). (1992). *Source book for creative problem solving.* Buffalo, NY: Creative Education Foundation.

Parnes, S. J., & Meadow, A. (1959). Effects of brainstorming instruction on creative problem solving of trained and untrained subjects. *Journal of Educational Psychology, 50*, 171–176.

Parnes, S. J., & Meadow, A. (1960). Evaluation of persistence of effects produced by a creative problem solving course. *Psychological Reports, 7*, 357–361.

Parnes, S. J., & Noller, R. B. (1972). Applied creativity: The creative studies project. Part II: Results of the two year program. *Journal of Creative Behavior, 6*, 164–186.

Reese, H. W., Parnes, S. J., Treffinger, D. J., & Kaltsounis, G. (1976). Effects of a creative studies program on structure of intellect factors. *Journal of Educational Psychology, 68*, 401–410.

Treffinger, D. J. (1980a). Fostering independence and creativity. *Journal for the Education of the Gifted, 3*, 214–223.

Treffinger. D. J. (1980b, May). Creative learning: What is it, and why is it important? *LTI Bulletin*, 6–7.

Treffinger, D. J. (1983). George's group: A creative problem solving facilitation case study. *Journal of Creative Behavior, 17*, 39–48.

Treffinger, D. J. (1986). Research on creativity. *Gifted Child Quarterly, 30*, 15–19.

Treffinger, D. J. (1991). Creative productivity: Understanding its sources and nurture. *Illinois Council for the Gifted Journal, 10*, 6–8.

Treffinger, D. J. (2000a). *Assessing CPS Performance* (2nd Ed.). Waco, TX: Prufrock Press.

Treffinger, D. J. (2000b). *The Creative Problem Solver's Guidebook* (3rd Ed.). Waco, TX: Prufrock Press.

Treffinger, D. J., & Huber, J. R. (1975). Designing instruction for creative problem solving: Preliminary objectives and learning hierarchies. *Journal of Creative Behavior, 9*, 260–266.

Treffinger, D. J., Isaksen, S. G., & Dorval, K. B. (1994). Creative learning and problem solving: An overview. In M. Runco (Ed.), *Problem finding, problem solving, and creativity* (pp. 223–226). Norwood, NJ: Ablex.

Treffinger, D. J., & McEwen, P. (1989). *Fostering independent, creative learning*. Buffalo, NY: DOK.

Treffinger, D. J., & Nassab, C. A. (2000). *Thinking tool lessons*. Waco, TX: Prufrock Press.

Treffinger, D. J., & Parnes, S. J. (1980). Creative problem solving for the gifted and talented. *Roeper Review, 2*, 31–32.

Treffinger, D. J., & Selby, E. C. (1993). Giftedness, creativity, and learning style: Exploring the connections. In R. Milgram, R. Dunn, & G. Price (Eds.), *Teaching and counseling gifted adolescents through their learning styles: An international perspective* (pp. 87–102). Westport, CT: Praeger.

Treffinger, D. J., & Sortore, M. R. (1990). Creative problem solving: The need, the process, the metamorphosis. *Journal of Secondary Gifted Education, 2*(2), 6–15.

Van Gundy, A. B. (1981). *Techniques of structured problem solving.* New York: Van Nostrand–Reinhold.

Van Gundy, A. B. (1984). *Managing group creativity: A modular approach to problem solving.* New York: American Management Association.

Van Gundy, A. B. (1987). Organizational creativity and innovation. In S. G. Isaksen, (Ed.), *Frontiers of creativity research: Beyond the basics* (pp. 358–379). Buffalo, NY: Bearly Limited.